D0049538

DATE DUE

BABE DIDRIKSON ZAHARIAS

BABE DIDRIKSON ZAHARIAS

Driven to Win

NANCY WAKEMAN

Lerner Publications Company • Minneapolis

To my mother, Frances M. Wakeman,
for her support and inspiration

I would like to thank members of the Didriksen family for talking with me: Dr. Greg Cole, Jackie Didriksen, and especially Ron Didriksen; Joe Shamburger and Carol Williford for letting me look through Babe's scrapbooks; Laura Hayes for her help in the beginning; Peggy Kirk Bell and Thad Johnson for talking with me. A special thanks to Sandy Wilson Kleine for making me feel welcome in Beaumont; David Montgomery for helping me in the Tyrrell Memorial Library. Thanks to my friends for their continued support and encouragement; Mary Robinson for helping with the submission process; the Wednesday Morning Writing Group and the Pumpkin Patch Writing Group for listening to this story and for their editorial expertise. Thanks to my editor, Dawn Miller, for her support.

Lerner Publications Company
A Division of Lerner Publishing Group
241 First Avenue North
Minneapolis, MN 55401 U.S.A.

Web site: www.lernerbooks.com

Library of Congress Cataloging-in-Publication Data

Wakeman, Nancy.
    Babe Didrikson Zaharias : driven to win / Nancy Wakeman.
        p. cm.
    Includes bibliographical references and index.
    Summary: a biography of the multi-talented female athlete, discussing the different sports in which she competed and her part in creating the first women's professional golf circuit.
    ISBN 0-8225-4917-4 (alk. paper)
    1. Zaharias, Babe Didrikson, 1911–1956—Juvenile literature.
    2. Athletes—United States—Biography—Juvenile literature.
    3. Women athletes—United States—Biography—Juvenile literature.
    4. Athletes. [1. Zaharias, Babe Didrikson, 1911–1956. 2. Women Biography.] I. Title.
    GV697.Z26W35 2000
    796.352'092
    [B]—dc21   99-13335

Manufactured in the United States of America
1 2 3 4 5 6 – JR – 05 04 03 02 01 00

Contents

By the time she was twenty-one years old, Babe had set numerous sports records.

ONE

A Memorable Performance

1932

On a hot summer day in July 1932, a taxicab screeched to a stop in front of Dyche Stadium in Evanston, Illinois. A slim, muscular young woman wearing a bright yellow tracksuit jumped out and ran into the sports arena. Babe Didrikson had arrived just in time.

She had been kept awake the night before by stomach pains, which a hotel doctor had told her were caused by nervousness. Babe had dozed off and on all night and then overslept in the morning. Worried that she would be too late to compete in the American Athletic Union (AAU) women's national track-and-field championships, Babe had run out of the hotel, hailed a taxicab, and changed into her tracksuit in the cab.

In the stadium, more than two hundred female athletes—representing twenty teams—nervously waited for the competition to begin. Dressed in their bright team colors, the women on each team stood clumped together, whispering to each other. As Babe moved through the crowd of athletes, a few of the women smiled or glanced at her, but no one approached her or offered words of encouragement.

Babe stood by herself, swung her arms, and tried to warm up. At twenty-one, she was an outstanding competitor who had won medals, broken records, and dazzled everybody with her athletic ability. She was ready to win every event she had entered and didn't hesitate to tell the other athletes. Babe had come to the AAU women's nationals as a one-woman team, representing the Golden Cyclones of Dallas, Texas.

The Golden Cyclones were a group of female athletes who played softball and basketball, and who competed at track-and-field meets. The Employers Casualty Insurance Company sponsored them. Babe had been working for Employers Casualty and competing for the Golden Cyclones for two years. As the time for the AAU meet approached, her coach, "Colonel" Melvin J. McCombs, studied women's track-and-field records from all over the United States and compared them to Babe's best efforts. When Babe asked him if the Golden Cyclones were going to compete in Evanston, his answer surprised her.

"I think if you enter enough different events and give your regular performance, you can do something that's never been done before. I believe we can send you up there to represent Employers Casualty Company, and you can win the national championship for us all by yourself," he said.

There was more at stake than the national championship, however. That summer, the AAU women's national track-and-field championships were combined with the tryouts for the U.S. Olympic team. The athletes who placed first, second, and third in each event would represent the United States at the Summer Olympics in Los Angeles.

Babe knew she was the best at what she did. Her natural athletic ability and her willingness to learn and to practice what she was taught had led her to many victories. But on that July day in Evanston, even she was nervous.

Dyche Stadium was packed with excited spectators. Thousands of people had come to the university town to watch the competition. As the announcer called the name of each team, groups of twenty or more women ran to the center of the stadium. Babe waited impatiently. At last the announcer called out, "The Golden Cyclones from Dallas, Texas!"

Babe, second from left, *competing in the 80-meter hurdles at the American Athletic Union (AAU) women's national meet*

Babe grinned, waved her arms over her head, and ran onto the field. The crowd greeted the one-woman team with a tremendous roar. "It brought out goose bumps all over me," Babe later recalled. Her nervousness vanished. She loved to compete and was ready to win. She would later remember that day in her autobiography: "It was one of those days in an athlete's life when you know you're just right. You feel you could fly. You're like a feather floating in air."

Babe was entered in eight of the ten events: 80-meter hurdles, shot put, broad jump, high jump, 100-yard dash, discus, javelin, and baseball throw. She raced from event to event. "For two and a half hours, I was flying all over the place," Babe said. "I'd run a heat in the 80-meter hurdles, and then I'd take one of my high jumps. Then I'd go over to the broad jump and take a turn at that. Then they'd be calling me to throw the javelin or put the eight-pound shot." Officials held up events until she was ready and gave her extra minutes to rest between each competition. By the end of the day, Babe's performance had lived up to her bragging.

Babe won five of the events she entered, and tied for first in another. Although she rarely threw the eight-pound shot put, she surprised everybody by winning that competition with a throw of 39 feet, 6¼ inches. She shattered the women's world record by throwing the javelin 139 feet, 3 inches—breaking her previous world record by 6 feet. In the baseball throw, she increased her own record with a toss of 272 feet, 2 inches. She flew over the 80-meter hurdles in 11.9 seconds, and also won the broad jump with a leap of 17 feet, 6 inches. Babe tied Jean Shiley for first place in the high jump. They both broke the world record with jumps of 5 feet, 3³⁄₁₆ inches. Babe also took fourth place in the discus throw. The only event in which Babe did not place was the 100-yard dash.

At the end of the day, meet officials added all the points. Babe was the winner! With a total of 30 points, she had won the AAU championship for the Golden Cyclones. The twenty-two members of the Illinois Women's Athletic Club took second place, with 22 points.

Babe was excited and proud. In less than three hours, she had won six gold medals, set four world records, won the AAU championship for her team, and secured a place on the U.S. Olympic women's track-and-field team. She strolled around the stadium, playing her harmonica and talking to reporters. The sportswriters were always looking for a good story, and Babe loved to talk about herself. One reporter wrote that her victory at Dyche Stadium was "the most amazing series of performances ever accomplished by any individual, male or female, in track-and-field history."

Babe described her parents as "strictly sweet."

TWO

Born to Play Sports

1911–1925

$\mathbf{B}$abe's father, Ole Didriksen, was a seafarer and ship's carpenter. Her mother, Hannah Marie Olsen, was considered one of the best skiers and ice skaters in Bergen, Norway. Ole and Hannah married, settled in Oslo, and began to raise a family. In the early years of the twentieth century, life was hard in Norway and there were few opportunities for young people. Ole found work as a ship's carpenter, but he was away from home for long periods on ocean voyages. Like many other Europeans, the Didriksens dreamed of immigrating to the United States and providing a better life for their children.

On one of his voyages, Ole sailed into Port Arthur, a bustling port on the Gulf Coast of Texas. The town was hot, humid, and smelled of oil. Tall oil derricks dotted the flatland. To Ole Didriksen, Port Arthur looked like the kind of town where a hard-working person could succeed. When he returned to Norway, he told Hannah he had found the perfect place to raise their family.

In 1905 Ole settled in Port Arthur and worked for three years as a cabinetmaker and furniture refinisher to satisfy immigration requirements and to prove he could support a family. In 1908 he sent for Hannah and their three children: Dora, Esther Nancy, and Ole Jr. In Texas the Didriksen family grew. The twins Lillie and Louis were born in 1909, Mildred Ella (Babe) arrived on June 26, 1911, and Arthur followed in 1915.

Ole put his carpentry skills to work and built a sturdy two-story house for his seven children. About the time Mildred Ella was born, the Didriksens moved into their new house. They didn't have many years to enjoy their new home, though. A few hours after Arthur was born, one of the worst hurricanes in history hit the Gulf Coast of Texas. Howling winds uprooted trees and lifted the roofs off houses. Huge waves rolled over the land, smashing buildings and drowning people. The Didriksen house remained standing, but the family lost everything else—furniture, clothing, and dishes. Even the chickens were washed away by the storm.

Ole, Hannah, and the children packed up and moved a few miles inland to Beaumont. They settled in a house on Doucette Street in a rough, rundown part of town near the Magnolia Oil Refinery. The refinery loomed over the town, and steam and smoke were always pouring out of its chimneys and smokestacks. Trolley tracks ran down the middle of the streets.

Athletically talented, the Didriksen children were always outside roller-skating, swimming in the Neches River, or playing baseball. Ole Didriksen encouraged his children in their physical activities. He made barbells from broom handles and flatirons, and he built a gym in the backyard. The gym was for the boys, but Mildred Ella and her sister Lillie worked out on it too.

"Before I was even into my teens I knew what I wanted to do with my life," Babe said, "I wanted to be the best athlete that ever lived." At an early age, Mildred Ella had tremendous self-confidence. Her body always did what she told it to do, and she excelled at any sport she played.

Even when she was very young, Mildred Ella could run faster and throw a ball farther than most boys. The great baseball player Babe Ruth was a hero to many people then. Because she was the youngest girl in her family, Mildred Ella's nickname was "Baby." When she began hitting home runs in baseball games, the other kids would say, "She's a regular Babe Ruth. We'll call her Babe."

Babe loved competing in sports. Outgoing and friendly, she was a natural leader at school and on the playground. She organized her own baseball team and played pitcher, third base, and shortstop. Basketball was another favorite. Babe would watch the high school girls practice and beg them to let her play.

Babe liked to be different or do things that were different. When she enrolled in school, her last name was spelled "Didrikson" by mistake. She liked the mistake and used that spelling for the rest of her life.

She was never interested in dolls and spent most of her time playing games with boys. But she didn't like being pushed around, and tempers sometimes exploded on the playground. She would often use her fists to settle an argument.

With her sister Lillie and her brother Arthur, Babe roamed the streets of Beaumont looking for adventure and excitement. Some of their games were dangerous. Babe and Lillie sometimes jumped on and off the freight trains that rumbled through town. On Halloween they soaped the trolley tracks that ran down Doucette Street. When the streetcars slid to a stop on the slippery tracks, Babe would jump on the back and disconnect the trolley pole from its power wire. The driver would have to get out and reconnect the pole. One

Babe, Arthur, and Lillie (left to right) *often wandered around Beaumont in search of adventure.* Opposite page: *Ole and Hannah Didriksen created a warm and loving environment for their family. Ole,* back row, *is pictured with five of their children. Babe is in the front row, center.*

time, Babe slipped in the mud and was nearly crushed by the streetcar.

Life in Beaumont was not all fun and games for Babe and her brothers and sisters. The Didriksens had to work hard. Ole had trouble finding carpentry jobs, so he returned to sea several times to support his family. Hannah Didriksen worked as a practical nurse and took in laundry. All the children had jobs. When Babe was in the seventh grade, she took her first after-school job at a fig-packing plant for thirty cents an hour. Then she found a better-paying job in a gunnysack factory, sewing bags for a penny apiece. With her excellent hand and eye coordination, Babe was one of the fastest workers. She made sixty-seven cents an hour, kept a nickel or a dime, and gave the rest to her mother. Babe's jobs didn't diminish her desire to play sports, though. With permission from her boss, she would often slip out of work for games and make up the time later.

All of the children helped with chores at home. On laundry day, each of the girls had specific things to iron. "My job was to iron the boys' khaki shirts and pants," Babe said. "With three or four for each boy every week, that got kind of rough." There were twenty-eight windows on the porch to be washed every Saturday, as well as the floors and woodwork. Hannah Didriksen expected all of her children to scrub the floors on their hands and knees. But when it was Babe's turn to wash the kitchen floor and her mother wasn't looking, Babe would tie scrub brushes to her feet and skate around on the soap suds.

Babe was an energetic and enthusiastic worker, but sports were more important to her than chores or errands. One day her mother sent her to the store to buy some meat for dinner and asked her to return as quickly as possible. On the way home Babe found a ball game. "I stopped to watch for a minute," she said, "and the next thing I knew I was in there playing myself. I laid the package of meat down on the ground. I was only going to play for a couple of minutes, but they stretched into an hour. Along came Momma down the street looking for me. I said, 'I got the meat, Momma. It's right here.' Then I looked where I'd left it, and there was a big dog eating up the last of that meat."

Even though money was always scarce in the Didriksen household, Hannah and Ole succeeded in creating a warm and loving family life for their children. But there was also order and discipline. Broken rules were met with immediate punishment. Babe received more than her share of spankings and extra chores. She remembered her parents as being "strictly sweet," though, with their punishment tempered by love.

Once, Hannah had made Babe a new dress. Babe wore it to school, played in it, and tore it. When she arrived home, Hannah was preparing supper, limping on a painfully swollen ankle that she had sprained days earlier. She lost her temper when she saw the torn dress. "She started after me, trying to run on that ankle," Babe wrote later. "I said, 'Momma, don't run. I'll wait for you.' She came up to me and was going to spank me. Then she looked at me and began to laugh. She said, 'I can't whip you.'"

Babe was nearly always outside playing sports and games. Although she was a hearty eater and loved the thick oatmeal and the Norwegian meatballs her mother made, she rarely came home unless she was very hungry or darkness had ended her games. There was one thing that could bring Babe home earlier: music. "Our whole family was musical," Babe said. "My brothers played the drums. Two sisters played the piano, and the other played the violin. Poppa could play violin too. Momma sang."

Babe played the harmonica. She had heard someone playing a harmonica in a radio talent show and decided to learn the instrument. She saved her money and bought her own, then she practiced and practiced. Playing the harmonica gave Babe pleasure throughout her life. The Didriksens often played music on their porch after dinner. They were so good that many of their neighbors would come outside to listen.

"It was just a wonderful family life we had there," Babe said of her childhood in Beaumont. Her neighbors called her a tomboy, but she didn't care. She loved playing sports and winning games. The Didriksens were a warm and affectionate family. Although they didn't approve of everything Babe did, they loved her and accepted her tomboy ways.

Babe's yearbook photo, 1928

THREE

Determined to Make the Team

1926–1930

When Babe entered Beaumont High School, she tried out for all the girls' teams: baseball, golf, swimming, tennis, volleyball, and basketball. Beatrice Lytel, who spent fifty years teaching physical education, said, "I saw possibly twelve thousand young women over those years. I observed them closely and trained a lot of them to be fine athletes. But there was never anyone in all those thousands who was anything like Babe. I never again saw the likes of her. Babe was blessed with a body that was perfect. I can still remember how her muscles flowed as she walked."

At fifteen Babe was barely 5 feet tall and weighed only 90 pounds. Even so, she won a place on almost every team. But when she tried out for the Miss Royal Purples, the Beaumont High School basketball team, the coach said she was too small. Ole Didriksen assured Babe she would soon grow and be tall enough to play on the girls basketball team. Everyone in the family seemed to stay small into their teens, only to shoot up in height as they grew older.

Babe didn't want to sit and wait until she had grown taller. She was determined to make the team. She used her study hours to practice basketball. "I'd show the teacher I had all my homework done and get excused from study hall," she said. Then she went to the boys' basketball coach, because she wanted to learn the more fundamental skills he could teach her. Babe asked endless questions—how to pivot (turn on one foot), how to shoot free throws, how to dribble—then she would practice on her own. Later, she would come back to the coach with more questions.

Babe was determined to excel at every sport she tried. She was never satisfied and always felt she could improve. Her desire to excel did not extend to her academic subjects, however. She was an average student and took only enough courses to remain eligible for sports.

Babe's passion for sports did not make her popular in high school. Her aggressiveness was considered unfeminine and her determined focus on sports unnatural. She made a few friends among the male and female athletes, but she didn't fit in with the popular crowd. The popular girls at Beaumont High School wore heels and silk stockings and styled their hair. Some of them may have played tennis or competed on the swimming team, but mostly they cheered for the Beaumont High football and baseball players.

During the 1920s and for many years before then, men were the ones who competed in sports and lived adventurous lives. A woman's place was considered to be in the home as an obedient daughter, or as a dedicated wife and mother.

There were women who were exceptions to this rule. In 1890 the journalist Nellie Bly traveled around the world by herself. Newspaper headlines of the day celebrated her trip as the first "Tour of the World by an Unattended Woman." Eleanora Sears excelled in many sports, including sailing, swimming, and squash. She won more than 240 trophies in amateur competition and four national amateur tennis titles between 1911 and 1917. In August 1926, Gertrude Ederle was the first woman to swim the English Channel, and she set a record doing it. These women were unusual.

In the early years of the twentieth century, there was a growing interest in women's sports. Basketball was very popular, and by 1920 most public schools had basketball teams for girls. In 1920 the United States sent a women's swimming team—its first women's team in any sport—to the Olympic Games. In that same year, after decades of protest and struggle, women in the United States won the right to vote. But the fact that women could vote, play on basketball teams, and participate in the Olympics did little to change social attitudes. The prevailing opinion was that women were supposed to be "good girls" who stayed home and quietly obeyed their fathers and husbands.

Babe wasn't quiet. Sometimes her teachers had to reprimand her for talking in class. On the playing field or basketball court she always wanted to win, and she had a temper. By high school, Babe had stopped using her fists to fight back; she used words. Babe began to brag about herself.

When she wanted to kick for the football team, she went to the football coach and said, "I can beat Raymond [the team's kicker] all to little bits and pieces at kicking." Babe lived up to her bragging. She kicked the ball farther and straighter than Raymond did, but the coach knew the school board and the high school sports league would never allow Babe to play on the team with her male classmates.

Not only did Babe's confidence and her passion for sports make her different; she also looked different. She hated "all that sissy stuff"—the high heels, perms, and stockings that the popular girls wore. She wore her hair short, with bangs

The Beaumont High School girls basketball team in 1929. Babe is in the front row, second from the left.

cut straight across her forehead. At school she wore denim skirts, socks, and flat shoes. Her favorite clothes were boys' pants and shirts.

While most of the high school girls were dating, Babe was too busy trying to be the best at every sport she tried. A boy was someone to talk with about the latest baseball averages, or someone to beat in competition. Most of the Beaumont High School students called her freak or toughie. The only times they cheered for Babe were when she was scoring points for her team.

Babe wasn't deterred by the attitudes of her schoolmates. She continued to practice her basketball shots and played on every team she could. She knew she was the best athlete at

Beaumont High School, and she believed that someday she was going to be the best athlete in the world.

Babe's family continued to support her athletic pursuits. Ole Didriksen liked to read the sports pages of the newspaper and talk to his children about the famous athletes of the day. One morning he started talking about the runners who were going to compete in the 1928 Olympic Games in Amsterdam, the capital of the Netherlands. Babe remembered that conversation in her autobiography.

> "Next year I'm going to be in the Olympics myself," I said.
> Poppa said, "No, Babe, you can't. You'll have to wait four years."
> I said, "Well, why? Why can't I be in it next year?" And he explained to me that the Olympic Games were held four years apart.

Babe immediately recruited her sister Lillie and began practicing for the Olympics. She jumped the hedges along their block. Lillie ran with her, but on the sidewalk. Lillie was a fast runner and had an advantage because she could run steadily while Babe had to jump. Eventually Babe was able to catch her and sometimes beat her.

There were seven hedges between the Didriksens' house and the corner grocery store. One hedge was higher than the others and interfered with Babe's practicing, so she asked the owners if they would cut it level with the others. They did.

Babe's constant basketball practice eventually paid off. When she was in her junior year, she won a place on the Miss Royal Purples. Her father was right. By the time she was seventeen, Babe had caught up with some of the other girls on the basketball team. She was 5 feet, 7 inches tall and weighed 128 pounds.

Babe quickly became the star of the team. She out-dribbled her opponents, ran faster than any other player on the court, and usually scored when she had the ball. In 1928 the editors of the *Pine Burr,* the Beaumont High School yearbook, wrote, "[Babe] plays with a grace and ease rivaling that of a dancer to tally goal after goal for the Purple during the season." The other players on the team complained that she didn't pass the ball enough. Babe didn't understand why they complained. When she was on the court, the Miss Royal Purples always won.

As the team won game after game, Babe began to attract attention. Her name appeared in newspapers across Texas. She made the all-city and all-state basketball teams. Babe enjoyed her growing fame and loved reading about herself in the papers. She cut out the articles and started a scrapbook.

During the 1920s, basketball was the most popular team sport for women, especially in the South and Midwest. It was a fast and exciting game and large crowds came to watch the high school teams play. But despite the popularity of high school basketball, there were few opportunities for female athletes beyond high school. Few colleges had basketball teams, strong athletic programs for women, or athletic scholarships.

Industrial basketball leagues for women were scattered all around the country. Sponsored by businesses, civic groups, and churches, the industrial teams were intensely competitive. Winning squads attracted many fans and were glorified in the sports pages of the local papers.

One day a scout from one of these industrial teams was at a basketball game between the Miss Royal Purples and a team from Houston. The scout was Colonel Melvin J. McCombs, a former army officer who worked for Employers

Casualty Insurance Company in Dallas and managed the company's sports program for women. McCombs had come to the game to scout the Houston team, but he couldn't keep his eyes off Babe. Babe was small compared to the Houston players McCombs had come to watch, but she was quick. She ran circles around the other team and outshot them. She scored 26 points by herself, and Beaumont won the game. McCombs was impressed. After the game, he introduced himself to Babe and asked if she would like to play on a big-time basketball team.

"Boy, would I! Where?" Babe said. McCombs offered her a secretarial job at Employers Casualty and a spot on the company basketball team, the Golden Cyclones. Babe's excited teammates crowded around to offer their congratulations.

Babe was in her last semester of high school, and even though she was old enough to drop out without her parents' permission, she sought their approval to pursue the opportunity in Dallas. McCombs drove Babe and Ole Didriksen, who had been at the game, home to Beaumont and had dinner with the whole family.

"[Babe] wanted to go in the worst way," her sister Lillie said. Their parents—especially Hannah—raised objections. They believed education was the key to a good life and a prosperous future. McCombs pointed out that the $75 a month offered by Employers Casualty would come to $900 a year— a good salary for a working woman in 1930. A skilled typist averaged $624 a year.

After McCombs left, the Didriksens discussed the offer. They worried about letting Babe drop out of school, even for a job that paid a good salary. The United States was suffering from the effects of a stock market crash that had occured just months earlier. Banks and businesses were failing, millions of workers faced unemployment, and the country was full of homeless and starving people.

Hannah Didriksen cried and thought of even more reasons why Babe shouldn't leave home. Babe was her youngest daughter. What would she do without Babe's company and her help with the housework? The Didriksens didn't own a car, and Dallas was too far away. Ole Didriksen was the one who finally persuaded his wife to let Babe go. Money was always scarce in the Didriksen household, he told her, and Babe would be able to send some money home each month. He reminded his wife that they had come to the United States to provide their children with opportunities. Beaumont High School agreed to let Babe return in June to take her exams and graduate with her class.

Babe left home on February 17, 1930. "You never saw anybody more excited than I was that night at the railroad station in Beaumont, Texas," she wrote in her autobiography. "Here I was just a little old high school girl wanting to be a big athlete. And now I was getting a chance." Babe had never traveled far from home before. For her, the 275-mile trip to Dallas was like going to Europe. But she was too excited to feel homesick about leaving her family. She knew that her trip to Dallas was the beginning of a new life, her life as an athlete.

Babe even looked like a different person. Instead of her usual overalls and T-shirts, she wore a dress that she had made at school and a hat. She even carried a purse with all the money she had—$3.49, the change from her train ticket.

McCombs met Babe at the Dallas train station in a big, yellow Cadillac that he used for driving the athletes to games. When he introduced her to the other players on the team, Babe had never met so many tall women with such big hands and feet. Even so, she refused to be intimidated by them.

One player approached Babe and said, "What position do you think you're going to play?"

"What do *you* play?" Babe answered.

"I'm the star forward."

"Well," Babe said, "that's what I want to be."

The same evening Babe arrived in Dallas, she was on the basketball court playing center-forward for the Golden Cyclones against Sun Oil Company, the defending national champions. The Sun Oil team knew of Babe's reputation and tried to keep her from shooting. "They started hitting me that night, and they kept it up the whole season. If one guard fouled out against me, they'd send in another one," she wrote in her autobiography.

Babe was unruffled by the Sun Oil team. She was a fierce competitor and was willing to put up with rough play in order to win. She managed to break away from her opponents and shoot some baskets. The Golden Cyclones won, 48 to 18. Babe played the entire game and scored fourteen points. The next day Babe wrote to her friend Tiny Scurlock, a sportswriter for the *Beaumont Journal,* whom she had come to know through his coverage of her games.

> Dear Tiny,
> Played my first game last night, and I never before practiced with them and they say that I was the girl that they have been looking for.

Babe earned money working as a secretary for Employers Casualty while playing on the company's sports team, the Golden Cyclones.

FOUR

Athlete in Training

1930–1932

Employers Casualty became Babe's family away from home. McCombs found her a room in a boardinghouse in the same neighborhood as her Golden Cyclones teammates. The athletes all ate together at the house of the assistant basketball coach, paying fifteen cents for breakfast and thirty-five cents for dinner. Sometimes they ate at the lunch counter of a local drugstore. "The guy at the soda fountain would never charge for my coke," Babe said. "He'd say, 'How about another one, champ?' That made me feel real good, because I wasn't any champ then."

Babe's rent was five dollars a month, and each month she sent $45 to her family in Beaumont. She watched her remaining $25 carefully. She had one pair of shoes and didn't spend any money on clothes. Sometimes one of her teammates would give her an old dress, which she would cut up and make into a skirt. To save carfare, McCombs drove Babe and her teammates to and from work.

Babe was successful in almost everything she did in Dallas. As a secretary, she was cheerful and efficient. After work she trained and competed with the other women. Few people in Dallas looked with disapproval at a woman who

Babe's natural athletic ability allowed her to excel at nearly every sport she tried.

competed in athletics. At last Babe was not regarded as weird or freakish, but was instead supported and praised for her dedication to sports.

Employers Casualty received much publicity for its sports teams, especially when the Golden Cyclones won. The company provided its athletes with the best coaching and equipment it could find. Flexible work schedules gave the athletes plenty of time to play sports. In addition to playing basketball, they competed in tennis, swimming, baseball, and diving. Babe excelled at them all.

"I didn't care too much for just swimming, but I did go for that fancy diving. I won diving events in swimming meets, and I honestly think I could have qualified for the Olympic swimming team if I had concentrated on it," she said with her usual confidence.

Babe continued to lead the Golden Cyclones to victories in basketball. But she was not satisfied with just winning. After two weeks of playing with the Golden Cyclones, she decided she wanted to be All-American. Being named All-American would rank her with the best players in the country. She wrote to her friend Tiny Scurlock:

> We have two All-American guards and two All-American forwards on our team and Mr. McCombs said that he would have three All-American guards and three All-American forwards before the season is over, so Tiny, I am up here now and that is what I am going to be, just watch and see.

In May the Golden Cyclones made it to the national basketball championships in Wichita, Kansas. There, they lost the title game to Sun Oil by one point. Babe scored 210 points in five games and was voted All-American at forward. In a few short months she had become the star of her team.

When scouts from other teams saw what an outstanding player Babe was, they tried to lure her away from the Golden Cyclones with offers of money. She was tempted; she liked having money, and her family always needed it.

In addition, some of the other women on the team were jealous of Babe. In her drive to be the best, Babe overshadowed her teammates as well as her opponents. She loved to be at center stage. Her bragging and me-first attitude irritated the other members of the Golden Cyclones. One of her teammates said, "Babe had great strength. She was born to run, to jump . . . she was good, she was fast, she could hit the basket. But . . . she was out for Babe . . . , just Babe."

Babe tried to act as though she didn't care about her popularity with her teammates, but their resentment bothered her. She later confided in her friend Tiny Scurlock:

> Heck Tiny, if I get me another letter from Wichita, Kansas, I'm gonna take it. Because I would like it better there. These girls here are just like they were in Beaumont High School. Jealous and more so because they are all here and trying to beat me. But they can't do it.

McCombs wasn't going to let jealousy or personality con-
flicts destroy his championship team. He recognized Babe's
athletic genius, but he also felt she needed help developing
her potential. Babe got a raise, extra time off, and extra coaching to keep her on the Golden Cyclones.

When the basketball season ended in May, McCombs
wanted his players to stay in shape. He especially wanted to
keep Babe from becoming too restless, so he took her to a
track-and-field meet. Despite her early fascination with hur-
dling hedges, it was the first time she had attended a meet.
McCombs had to explain some of the events to her.

"What's that?" Babe asked, when she saw a big stick
lying on the ground.

"It's a javelin. You throw it like a spear," McCombs said,
showing her the basic motion. Babe picked up the javelin and
tried it. As she threw it, the javelin slapped her back and raised
a welt. That didn't stop her; she threw it again and again. Then
she watched a hurdle race and was reminded of all the hedge
jumping she had done in Beaumont. "I liked the looks of that
event better than almost anything else," Babe said.

When he saw how Babe took to track and field,
McCombs knew he had found a way to keep her occupied
during the summer. All the Golden Cyclones were interested
in the sport. Babe stood out from the others by quickly adapt-
ing to many events. She was equally skilled at throwing the
discus and clearing the high jump. She mastered the skills for
each event, then practiced constantly.

As their first track-and-field meet approached, the Golden
Cyclones members began to pick different events to enter. One
woman wanted to throw the discus, another the javelin. When
it was Babe's turn to choose she asked, "Colonel, how many
events are there in track and field?"

"Why, Babe, I think there are about nine or ten," the Colonel replied.

"Well I'm going to do them all," she said.

Practicing with the team for one or two hours every afternoon wasn't enough for Babe. She trained until dark—long after supper. She ran in the park. Then she practiced step timing for the broad jump and high jump and practiced arm motions for the shot put and discus.

The night before her first meet, Babe practiced even harder. She spent hours working on the broad jump and high jump, then she sprinted 440 yards. She collapsed at the finish

Babe trained for many hours to prepare herself for the AAU championships.

line, saw stars, and lay on the ground for almost half an hour. When she told McCombs about it the next morning, he gently scolded her. "What are you trying to do, kill yourself?" he said.

Babe's constant practice paid off. She entered four events and won them all. That summer the Golden Cyclones traveled to track meets around the South. Wherever the team went, Babe won gold medals and set records. By the end of her first season, Babe had set national records in the javelin and baseball throws. She also held southern regional records in those events as well as in the high jump, the long jump, and the eight-pound shot put.

When the basketball season resumed, Babe again played brilliantly. At a time when 20 points for an entire team was considered good, Babe scored an average of 33 points a game. She led her team to the AAU championship in 1931 and was once again selected to the all-American team.

Babe's outstanding performances in basketball and track and field brought her more attention from the press. The *Dallas Morning News* called Babe the "ace of the local Golden Cyclones" and wrote that she was probably "the world's outstanding all-round feminine athlete."

Babe was young and inexperienced, and she believed what she read about herself in the paper. She became even more self-confident. Some of her teammates thought she became more arrogant and self-centered with every medal she won.

Babe continued playing with the Golden Cyclones in 1932. She hit home runs for the softball team, gave diving exhibitions, and played tennis doubles with her teammates. She led her basketball team to second place in the AAU championships and was named All-American for the third time.

Babe knew some of her teammates resented her athletic success and the attention she received. When their snubs bothered her, she retaliated by gossiping about them. She continued to maintain her swaggering, tough-girl image. When a reporter once tried to ask if Babe wore, in her words, "girdles, brassieres, and the rest of that junk." Babe replied sharply. "The answer is no. What do you think I am, a sissy?" Babe liked being different. At a time when women were expected to look soft and round, she was muscular and lean. Babe continued to wear her hair short and straight when curls were the norm.

Twenty-one-year-old Babe Didrikson was a star athlete at the top of her form. "I know I'm not pretty," she said, "but I do try to be graceful." On the basketball court or the playing field, Babe certainly was the most graceful female athlete ever seen. She tried to put the jealousy of her teammates behind her as she concentrated on her next challenge: winning the AAU women's national track-and-field competition in Evanston, Illinois.

FIVE

Olympic Champion

1932

After Babe's amazing victories in Illinois, the sports-writers predicted her teammates would elect her captain of the U.S. Olympic women's track-and-field team. However, while Babe's teammates admired her athletic ability, they resented the special treatment she received at the AAU meet. She had been allowed to enter as many events as she wanted, while they were restricted to three events each. The judges sometimes gave her extra time to rest between events. Furthermore, the other athletes disliked Babe's penchant for calling attention to herself whenever possible. They were tired of her loud harmonica playing and constant bragging.

For captain of the team, they chose Jean Shiley, who had tied with Babe in the high jump at the AAU women's national track-and-field championships. Babe shrugged it off. She had more important things to think about, such as winning medals at the Olympics.

Seventeen women had won places on the U.S. Olympic women's track-and-field team. They traveled directly from Evanston, Illinois, to Los Angeles, California, by train. From their private rail car hung a red, white, and blue banner

Crowds of people began arriving in Los Angeles the day before the Olympic 1932 Games.

proclaiming them members of the U.S. Olympic Team. As the train traveled across the country, many people turned out to wave at the athletes. Most of the women on the team talked, played cards, or just sat and watched the scenery. Few of the athletes had done much traveling, and the trip was exciting for them.

Babe was full of energy. She wanted to stay in shape, so she jogged up and down the aisles and stretched out her legs on the backs of seats. Her teammates told her to take it easy and relax. Babe responded with practical jokes—putting ice down their backs or pulling pillows out from under their heads as they slept—which irritated them even further.

When the train stopped in Denver, Colorado, the athletes had a chance to stretch and practice at a local stadium. One aspect of the stop disappointed Babe. "I was looking forward to seeing the Mile High City," she wrote in her autobiography. "I didn't realize the slogan came from the fact that Denver is a mile above sea level. It sounds silly now, but I expected to see a city that was built a mile up in the air."

From Denver, the train traveled straight through to California. Babe loved everything about Los Angeles and was excited about the opportunity to compete against the best athletes in the world. Two thousand athletes from thirty-nine countries ventured to Los Angeles, the movie capital of the world, to compete in the Olympic Games. They became the stars of the moment. Movie actors wanted to pose for photographs with them. Newspapers were full of stories about them.

Sportswriters competed with each other to glamorize the athletes and turn them into larger-than-life figures. Sports became entertainment, an escape from the worries of daily life. People read about athletes in the paper instead of dwelling on the poverty and unemployment that continued to plague the United States during the Great Depression.

The public wanted to know what the athletes ate, how long they slept at night, and the secrets of their success. Babe was fresh from her victories in Illinois and eager to talk about herself. Her Texas drawl and her witty, unpredictable answers

Members of the 1932 U.S. Olympic women's track-and-field team, as they arrived in Los Angeles. Babe is pictured in the back row, third from the right.

captivated reporters. When they asked about her "beauty diet," Babe said, "I eat anything I want, except greasy foods and gravy. That's just hot grease anyway, with flour and water in it."

The female athletes were allowed to enter only three events at the Olympics. When the reporters asked her how many medals she planned to win, Babe said, "I came out here to beat everybody in sight, and that's just what I'm going to do. Yep, I'm going to win the high jump . . . and set a world record. I don't know who my opponents are and, anyways, it wouldn't make any difference." Babe and her teammates enjoyed the attention from the press, but they had come to Los Angeles to work. They trained hard during the ten days before the opening ceremonies. Babe practiced her events—the javelin throw, the 80-meter hurdles, and the high jump.

On August 1, a sellout crowd of more than one hundred thousand spectators crowded into the Los Angeles Coliseum to watch the opening ceremonies of the Tenth Olympiad. The athletes paraded into the stadium, a huge white-robed choir sang "The Star-Spangled Banner," and thousands of doves were released and flew up into the hot air. The Olympic flame was lit, and the athletes took the Olympic oath. U.S. Vice President Charles Curtis, Los Angeles Mayor John C. Porter, and other dignitaries made speeches. The athletes stood in the hot sun and listened.

As the ceremony dragged on, Babe grew more and more uncomfortable. The women had to wear special dresses, stockings, and white shoes that the Olympic committee gave them. Babe was used to wearing socks and pants. "I believe that was about the first time I'd ever worn a pair of stockings," she said, "and as for those shoes, they were really hurting my feet." Babe slipped off her shoes and listened to the speeches in her stocking feet.

The individual events began the next day. Babe's first event, the javelin throw, wasn't scheduled until late afternoon. In the meantime, Babe waited and worried. She wanted to warm up, but there were so many people on the field that she was afraid to make her usual long throws. The javelin might hit someone. Instead, she made short throws toward the ground. When her javelin narrowly missed another athlete, Babe stopped practicing. She stretched, swung her arms, and tried not to be nervous about her lack of warm-up time.

The announcer finally called her name. Babe trotted out onto the field, and her worries disappeared. She grasped the javelin and concentrated on throwing it beyond the small flag that marked the record-setting throw of a woman on the German team. As Babe flung her arm forward, her hand slipped, and she felt a sharp pain in her shoulder. The javelin flew straight as an arrow, without its usual arc. It traveled 143 feet, 4 inches—well past the German's flag. The crowd roared. Babe had set Olympic and world records.

Babe's awkward throw had torn cartilage in her right shoulder, however. She said nothing about the painful injury and took her two remaining throws. Both were weak. Fortunately, nobody else could match Babe's first javelin throw, so she won the gold medal.

Reporters wanted to know about her new way of throwing the javelin. "No, I haven't got a new technique," Babe told them. "My hand slipped when I picked up the pole. It slid along about six inches and then I got a good grip again. And then I threw it and it just went."

Babe wanted to be the first woman to win three gold medals at the Olympic Games, so she was not going to let a shoulder injury stop her from entering the 80-meter hurdles. Two days after winning her gold medal in the javelin throw, she ran in the preliminary heats of the 80-meter hurdles. She won the first race in a world record-tying 11.8 seconds.

The day of the final race, Babe had one false start when she crossed the start line ahead of the gun, then she hesitated a split second after the gun to avoid another false start. She caught up with her teammate Evelyn Hall two hurdles from the finish line. Then they ran side by side to the end.

Officials were hard-pressed to say who had won. Films of the race show the two runners tied at the finish. Both women reached the finish line in 11.7 seconds, setting a world record. The judges huddled, then after much delay announced that Babe was the winner. The crowd in the stadium roared. Everyone had read stories about Babe in the newspapers and they liked the confident, colorful Texan. The excitement at the Games grew. Now Babe had two gold medals. Would she be the first woman in history to win three gold medals in track and field in a single Olympic year?

Babe's third and final event was the high jump. The only competitor she had to worry about was Jean Shiley. The two women had tied in the high jump and shared the world's record, set at the AAU women's nationals earlier in the summer.

When the competition began, Babe seemed unbeatable. She cleared the bar again and again. Finally, only Babe and Jean Shiley remained. The judges raised the bar to 5 feet, 5¼ inches. Both women cleared the bar and broke the world record. Then the judges raised the bar another inch—to 5 feet, 6¼ inches. "I took my turn," Babe said. "I went into my western roll, kicking up and rolling over. I just soared up there. I felt like a bird. I could see that bar several inches beneath me as I went across. I was up around five-ten, higher than I had ever been, and it was a sensation like looking down from the top of the Empire State Building."

Even though Babe, second from right, *and Evelyn Hall,* right, *both reached the finish line of the 80-meter hurdles in 11.7 seconds, Babe was declared the winner.*

When Babe landed, her foot struck one of the posts holding the crossbar, and the bar fell. She had missed the jump. The judges moved the bar back down to 5 feet, 5¼ inches for a runoff between the two athletes. They jumped, and again they both cleared the bar at that height. The judges huddled together and talked about Babe's style of jumping. Both women waited impatiently, ready to jump again.

Then the judges ruled Babe's jump to be a dive (which was illegal) because her head crossed over the bar before the rest of her body. According to the rules in 1932, jumpers had to bring their feet over the bar before their head. Babe's style was also unconventional: Jean Shiley and most other high jumpers used a scissors kick and cleared the bar in nearly a vertical position. Modern rules specify that jumpers can clear the bar in any fashion, as long as they take off from one foot.

Babe was furious. She had been jumping the same way all afternoon. If she was diving, she asked, why hadn't they disqualified her earlier? Event officials said they had not noticed her diving earlier. Babe stormed off the field. The gold medal went to Jean Shiley, while Babe was given the silver.

Sportswriters took Babe's side. Her jumps looked legal to them. Babe's second-place finish did not dampen the enthusiasm of her fans. The crowd in the stadium cheered loudly when Babe claimed her silver medal. Newspaper headlines proclaimed her victories from coast to coast. "Three Medals for Babe, World's Greatest Woman Athlete," proclaimed one. The sports pages were filled with stories of her triumphs.

Babe's Olympic victories were victories for all the citizens of the United States. The twenty-one-year-old had become a national celebrity. Grantland Rice, the most famous sportswriter of the day, invited Babe to play golf with him and some of his sportswriter friends. Babe was thrilled by the invitation, but nervous.

She had played some golf as a teenager, but she was not experienced, and her shots often went wild. In golf, players hit a small ball from the tee to a hole marked by a flag some distance away. They want to hit the ball into the hole—to "hole out"—in as few strokes as possible, because the lowest score for the course wins. On most eighteen-hole courses, a score in the low seventies is considered good.

Babe shot a 95 that afternoon. Even so, Grantland Rice and the other sportswriters praised her ability. "She is the longest hitter women's golf has ever seen, for she has a free, lashing style backed up with championship form and terrific power in strong hands, strong wrists, forearms of steel," Rice wrote.

That August afternoon was significant in Babe's life. She had thought about becoming a champion golfer, and receiving such praise from the foremost sportswriter of her day helped her decide.

When the Games were over, Babe returned to Texas. Employers Casualty paid her plane fare to Dallas. Local dignitaries, huge crowds, and marching bands greeted her. The city of Dallas gave her a huge ticker-tape parade. Her parents and her sister Lillie drove up from Beaumont and joined Babe on a ride through the city in a red limousine filled with roses. Babe's Golden Cyclones teammates formed an honor guard at each side of the car. People waved and threw confetti from the windows of buildings.

When Babe arrived in Beaumont, there were more festivities. She was given the key to the city. The high school band was called back from summer vacation to play in the victory parade. Babe and her parents rode through town in the fire chief's car. Members of the Miss Royal Purples marched alongside them. The mayor of Beaumont led the parade through the streets to the Didriksens' house. The tomboy who once roamed the streets of Beaumont had proven to everyone that she was the best athlete in the world.

SIX

Difficult Years

1932–1934

After the Olympic Games, Babe was one of the most famous personalities of the day. She made personal appearances and gave many interviews. Everyone wanted to know the secret of her success. "A lot of people get surprised because I have done so much winning against girls; shucks that's nothing," Babe told a reporter with her typical frankness. "I grew up running against boys and wrestling them. . . . it got so I could beat pretty near all of them, so why should people think it's great when I win from girls, most of whom never had any athletic training until they got into their teens—by which time I had played all the rough boys' games."

Being famous wasn't earning Babe any money, and she needed an income to support herself and to help her family. The Illinois Women's Athletic Club offered her $300 a month to join their team, but Babe didn't want to leave Texas. When she told Colonel McCombs about the offer, he raised her salary to $300 a month. She went back to work for Employers Casualty and back to playing basketball with the Golden Cyclones.

Babe was generous with her money. She sent home most of her salary and bought presents for everyone in her family—new clothing for her father, brothers, and sisters, and a new stove and icebox for her mother. Babe wasn't interested in new clothes, but she loved cars and she loved to drive. Within a few months of her Olympic victories, she bought a red Dodge coupe for herself.

Soon after she bought the car, her picture appeared in an advertisement for Dodge automobiles. She was quoted as saying, "Speed—unyielding strength—enduring stamina—that's the stuff that makes real champions, whether they're in the athletic arena or in the world of automobiles."

By AAU rules, amateur athletes could not earn money for playing sports or from promoting products. The AAU promptly suspended Babe for an indefinite length of time. She would not be allowed to play basketball, or any other sport, for the Golden Cyclones. Babe wrote telegrams to the AAU, angrily denying that she had authorized and profited from the advertisement. She had never said the words attributed to her, and the photograph had been used without her permission, she said. She insisted the car was not a gift—she was paying for it with her own money. The sports pages were full of the story of the wonder girl whose image was now tarnished by rumors of wrongdoing.

The dispute was finally settled when the automobile dealer who placed the advertisement backed up Babe's story. He showed the AAU a letter from him to an advertising agency that proved she hadn't known about the advertisement. The AAU immediately reinstated her as an amateur athlete. But Babe had had enough of the AAU and its rules and regulations. The incident soured Babe on amateur athletics and made her think seriously about the future. Many people told her she could make a lot of money if she turned professional. Babe liked the idea. Having money would mean she could buy the luxuries she never had as a child. She could also buy more gifts for her family.

In the midst of Babe's uncertainties about her future, she received some welcome news. The Associated Press named her Woman Athlete of the Year for 1932. She was thrilled.

In the end, Babe decided to turn professional. In the 1930s, however, there were very few women who made a living from sports. Babe played some tennis and golf, but she didn't play either sport well enough to compete with the best players. And even if she mastered them, most of the women's tournaments were for amateurs and didn't award prize money. Female athletes made their money by playing exhibition matches to display their talents or by promoting athletic clothing and equipment.

Babe knew that she had to keep her name in the public eye if she wanted to make money. If she were famous, people would pay to see her. She resigned from Employers Casualty and put her amateur career behind her. The Chrysler Motor Company, which had gotten her suspended from the AAU, promptly hired her to promote their cars. "They were sorry about what had happened, and they wanted to make it up to me," Babe said.

Traveling with her sister Esther Nancy, Babe went to Detroit and signed autographs at the Detroit Auto Show. She also entertained people by playing harmonica. The Chrysler executives were tickled.

Before long, Babe hired George T. Emerson, an advertising executive she met through Chrysler, as her agent. Emerson quickly booked Babe with theaters as a vaudeville act. She would entertain on stage in front of live audiences.

Her first stop was the Palace Theater in Chicago, where Babe's name stood four feet high in lights. She got top billing and the star's dressing room. On the first day, when Babe saw the crowd lined up outside the show, she panicked. But she soon took to the stage.

To open her act, Babe walked down the aisle dressed in a panama hat, a green knee-length jacket, and high heels. She sang a few songs, changed into track shoes, and peeled away her jacket to reveal a red, white, and blue tracksuit made of silk. She jogged on a treadmill, jumped a hurdle, hit plastic golf balls into the audience, and played harmonica.

Babe was a hit. The audiences loved her, and the show ran for a week. Babe enjoyed playing to the audiences too. Promoters offered her $2,500 a week to take the show to New York, but Babe was tired of performing four or five shows a day and spending all her time in a hotel or the theater. "I don't want the money if I have to make it this way," she told Esther Nancy. "I want to live my life outdoors. I want to play golf."

Babe set about making money her way. Emerson arranged for her to appear at various sporting events in New York. As always, Babe was confident she could defeat any opponent. Her first engagement was a billiards match against Ruth McGinnis, a champion pool player, who beat her soundly. But Babe was not discouraged. She went on to play in exhibition basketball games.

Despite her popularity with the crowds, Babe's opportunities quickly dwindled. Newspaper reporters had loved her when she won medals at the Olympic Games. But now the Games were over, and many of them wrote that competing in sports for money was acceptable for men and boys, but not for women or girls.

Babe returned home to Texas to plan her next move. With eighteen hundred dollars she had saved from her public appearances, Babe decided to dedicate the next few years to studying and practicing golf. She invited her parents and her sister Lillie to go to California with her and keep her company while she honed her game. In March 1933, they drove from Beaumont to Los Angeles in her famous Dodge coupe. "I have enough money to last me three years and I intend to win the women's amateur golf championship before those three years and my bankroll are gone," Babe told a reporter.

In Los Angeles, she met Stan Kertes, a golf pro who had many famous clients, such as the Marx Brothers and Bob

Babe, left, *tried her hand at pool, but lost to champion pool player Ruth McGinnis,* right.

Babe learned the game of golf under Stanley Kertes, an experienced golf pro. This photo of the two of them was taken in 1933.

Hope. He liked Babe's warmth and honesty and gave her free lessons and practice time at the driving range where he worked. Even with her natural athletic ability, Babe struggled with golf.

Most champion golfers begin playing by the age of ten. Although Babe had played a little golf in high school, she didn't immerse herself in the game until she was in her early twenties. She had to learn when to use each of the different kinds of clubs and how to hit the ball in certain situations. She had to practice many hours to get her swing to flow naturally.

Babe tackled golf with her usual discipline and drive. She practiced eight to ten hours a day and hit thousands of balls. When her hands blistered and bled, she bandaged and taped them and then hit more balls.

The money Babe had saved lasted only six months, but her constant practice had greatly improved her golf game during that time. When Babe's money ran out, she, Lillie, and her parents returned to Beaumont. Before long, Babe returned to her job at Employers Casualty. "Those people were wonderful to me," she said. "There must have been four or five times when I had to come back to them, and there was always a job for me at three hundred dollars a month."

Ole Didriksen fell ill that autumn, and Babe wanted extra money to help with the medical bills. She went back on tour, playing basketball on a team of four men and three women. "Babe Didrikson's All-Americans" traveled throughout the Midwest, driving over back roads during the day and playing local men's teams at night. Thousands of people came out to watch them play.

Babe stayed with her basketball team until the 1934 season ended. Then, determined to maintain her visibility as an athlete, she went to Florida to play in exhibition games with major league baseball teams during spring training. She pitched against the Boston Red Sox, the St. Louis Cardinals, and the Brooklyn Dodgers. She wasn't a great pitcher, but she loved joking around with the players. She even met her hero, Babe Ruth.

During her years on the road, Babe said that she earned forty-five to fifty thousand dollars. In the 1930s, that was good money.

Babe loved making money, but the years following the Olympics were exhausting and frustrating for her. Her father was often sick, and when her mother also became ill, Babe became the main breadwinner for her family. She didn't mind providing for her parents, but she wasn't happy.

The constant travel was hard on her, and she was dissatisfied with the direction of her career. Her reputation as an athlete was fading. Babe had become a symbol of the negative effects of sports on women. Mothers warned their daughters against turning out like Babe Didrikson. "Don't be a muscle moll," they said. Babe's popularity was waning, and she knew she must reclaim her fans.

Babe recaptured the attention of fans when she turned to golf.

SEVEN

Wonder Girl Once Again

1934–1937

In September 1934, Babe went home to Texas. "My name had meant a lot right after the Olympic Games, but it had sort of been going down since then. . . . I had to find some way to build up my name again," Babe said. She even considered becoming a tennis player. The shoulder injury she sustained during the Olympics hadn't completely healed, however, and it prevented her from getting off a powerful serve. Her golf swing was still fine, so Babe continued to practice golf.

When golf pro Bobby Jones played an exhibition in Houston, Babe went to watch him. "I was impressed by the way he stepped up there on the tee and slugged the ball. He was out to hit the ball just as hard as he could. And that's always been my kind of golf," she said. Watching her favorite golfer renewed Babe's desire to make a career in golf.

Babe returned to Employers Casualty and her secretarial job. Hoping to find some support for her golf career, she went to Homer Mitchell, the president of Employers Casualty, and talked to him about her dreams of being a professional golfer. He got her a membership at the Dallas Country Club and arranged for lessons with the club's pro, George Aulbach.

Despite the challenges that golf presented, Babe knew she had chosen her next sport well. It was upper-class and offered respectability that she wouldn't get with the vaudeville-type performances she had been staging.

Women had been playing amateur golf at country clubs in the United States since 1889. When Babe took up the sport, only one legitimate tournament was open to professional women golfers. Even so, competing in the many amateur tournaments would help her establish herself as a golfer.

Babe practiced with her usual determination and dedication. In November, she entered her first tournament, the Fort Worth Invitational, to see how much progress she had made. A reporter asked her how she thought she would do. "I think I'll shoot a 77," Babe said. She played her first round and won. Her score? 77.

The Texas papers were full of her triumph. "WONDER GIRL DEBUTS IN TOURNAMENT GOLF: TURNS IN 77 SCORE," one headline read. Babe lost a later round to a better golfer, but she was not disappointed. She knew her game wasn't perfect, and she hadn't expected to win.

After the Fort Worth Invitational, the golf tournament season wound down for the winter. Babe had accomplished her goal, though: She had tested herself in formal competition against experienced golfers. She had also learned how much work she needed to do in the off-season. Her next challenge would be the Texas Women's Amateur in April 1935. "No prize I've won either before or since, looked any bigger to me than the Texas Women's Golf Championship," Babe said in her autobiography. She went home to Dallas and began preparing herself for the tournament.

Babe devoted her weekends to playing golf. During the week, she practiced for three hours before work. During her lunch hour, she practiced putting and chipping on the carpet in her boss's office. After work, Babe hit ball after ball at the golf course, practicing every shot imaginable. She read from the rule book each night before falling asleep.

The wealthy society ladies who played amateur golf thought Babe was being pushy when she entered the Texas Women's Amateur. Her Olympic medals didn't mean anything to them. They considered her an upstart with no social connections or family money, and they disapproved of her travels around the country competing against men in baseball and basketball. They questioned her country-club membership and gossiped maliciously about her.

Not all the society crowd disliked Babe. R. L. and Bertha Bowen, two wealthy Texans who were influential in Texas golf, had seen her play. They were impressed with her determination and talent. When others scorned Babe, they befriended her. "It wasn't ladylike to be muscular. Of course, there's where her courage came in," Bertha Bowen said. " I never understood how she had the strength to overlook the snubs and the downright venom of a lot of women. She never talked ugly about anybody and she had every reason to. . . . But she never held a grudge."

Babe ignored the gossip and concentrated on her game. She won her first two matches at the Texas Women's Amateur, and also her quarterfinal match. The tournament was a major one on the golf circuit, and her victories attracted the attention of the press. Soon she had a gallery, or group of spectators, following her from hole to hole. When she won her semifinal match, the gallery cheered and sportswriters swarmed around her. One reporter from The Associated

Press wrote that Babe was "still America's wonder girl athlete and probably the most promising woman golf player in the United States."

Babe was glad to be called a wonder girl again, but she still had to beat Peggy Chandler to win the tournament. Chandler was a formidable opponent and popular with the country-club golf set. She had won the state championship once and had played in the finals two other times. Their match would be demanding. They would play eighteen holes in the morning and eighteen in the afternoon, for a total of thirty-six holes. They competed for holes—if one holed out with fewer strokes than

Babe, left, *and Peggy Chandler,* right, *at the Texas Women's Amateur golf tournament*

the other, she would win the hole. The golfer who won the most holes would win the match.

The day of the final match, the course was still soggy from the previous day's rain. Despite the conditions, Babe had a fantastic start. She beat Chandler by three strokes on the first hole. By the time they reached the twelfth hole, Babe was five holes ahead. Even though Peggy Chandler was behind, she played a steady game and did some fine putting.

Then Babe began to lose her focus. She seemed dazzled by Chandler's shots, and her own shots began to go wild. Her long drives landed in the rough, and her putts missed the cup. Babe lost her lead. At the end of the first eighteen holes, Chandler was ahead by one hole.

In the afternoon, the sun broke through the clouds and the course began to dry out. When Babe walked out onto the course to resume the match, she had regained her confidence. Chandler quickly forged ahead to a three-hole lead. Then Babe began to outdrive Chandler. Both golfers continued to play well, but Babe's drives often landed forty or fifty yards beyond Chandler's. When they reached the thirty-third hole, they each had won the same number of holes.

Chandler took three shots to reach the thirty-fourth green. Her third shot put the ball two feet away from the cup for a near-certain birdie (one stroke under par). Babe hit twice but wasn't on the green. Her ball had landed in a muddy rut beyond the green. "I said to myself, 'Now Babe, you can't make any more mistakes. You've got to take your time and play this one just right.'. . . I remembered the first rule of golf that everybody had told me: 'Look at the ball real good.' So I swung, and I did everything right, and dug that ball up there. . . . And then there was a roar, and the people behind me came rushing up, and somebody knocked me facedown into that muddy ditch. The ball had gone into the hole for an eagle." Babe's eagle (two strokes under par) gave her the lead. The two women played the thirty-fifth hole in the same number of strokes. On the last hole, Babe finished in four shots to Chandler's five. Babe won the tournament by two holes.

Newspapers all across the country reported Babe's latest victory. Babe was happy and excited. "I was on top of the world that day," she said. "I was rolling at last. . . . Now I was ready to shoot for the national championship." She planned to tour the country to compete in golf tournaments.

Babe didn't have long to enjoy her victory. Her championship had shaken up the polite world of country-club golf. To the Texas society women, Babe was a brash upstart who was too muscular and who hit the ball too far. The day after she won the tournament, the United States Golf Association (USGA)—the organization that sets the rules for amateur golf—began to receive complaints about Babe.

Someone from the Texas Women's Golf Association argued that Babe was a professional athlete because she had played basketball and baseball for money. And since Babe had been a professional in at least one other sport, she shouldn't be considered an amateur in golf. The USGA agreed and excluded her from all future amateur tournaments.

At first Babe was devastated. She had spent so much energy and time developing her golf game. But if she was angry with the Texas golfers, she kept it to herself. Instead, Babe contacted the USGA to try to regain her amateur standing. Many sportswriters and golfers spoke up for her. The Beaumont Country Club protested the ruling and asked for a hearing, but the USGA stood by its decision. There was only one tournament that she could enter—the Western Open. It was the only competition then open to women professionals.

After spending only a few months learning the game of golf, Babe won the Texas state women's golf championship in Houston. It was the second tournament in which she had ever competed.

Babe began looking for other opportunities. "When you get a big setback like that, there's no use crying about it," she said. "You just have to face your problem and figure out what to do next." She turned to the Bowens for advice.

"I was just furious at those people who had been so cutting to her," Bertha Bowen said. "The fact that she was poor and had no clothes did not mean she had to be ruled a professional." The Bowens did more than give Babe advice. Bertha Bowen made some phone calls and used her influence to change the Fort Worth Invitational into the Texas Open. That made two tournaments open to professional female golfers.

In June 1935, Babe entered the Western Open. She hit many of the 250-plus-yard drives that were becoming her trademark, but she lost in the quarterfinals. Babe was not discouraged. Other opportunities were opening for her.

The week of the Western Open, she announced that she had agreed to promote products of the Wilson Sporting

Goods Company for $5,000 a year. When a reporter asked her about the USGA decision, Babe was gracious. "Of course I was disappointed when they told me I couldn't compete as an amateur, but I admire them for barring me too," she said. "They were big enough to adhere to their rules. And as it all turned out, I'm very happy."

She also looked for other ways to learn more about golf and to make more money. In the summer of 1935, Babe teamed up with Gene Sarazen, the first golfer to win four major men's championships. They took a two-month tour of the Midwest, the East Coast, and New England. "Gene played the golf, and I put on the show," Babe said. She knew the crowds were there to see Gene Sarazen, because he had won many tournaments. Compared to Gene, Babe was a novice.

Babe wanted to be the best, and by touring with Sarazen, she had a chance to learn from one of the best. She watched everything he did and asked him questions. Then she practiced for hours. She was hitting drives of three hundred yards or more. No other woman, and not many men, could hit drives that long. Babe also learned how to deal with tricky situations, like water hazards and sand traps, on a golf course. Her golf game improved considerably and so did her finances. In addition to the money she received from Wilson, she made one hundred fifty dollars from the gate receipts every day she played with Sarazen.

Babe enjoyed herself on the tour. She liked to joke with Sarazen on the golf course. She would hit one of her long drives and then turn to him and say, "Don't you men wish you could hit a drive like that?"

Babe would also entertain the crowds who came to watch them play. "You all come closer now," she would say, in her best East Texas drawl. "Because you've heard of Walter

Hagen, you've heard of Bobby Jones, you've heard of Ben Hogan, but today you're looking at the best." Then she would show off her trick shots. She would put her foot in front of the ball, hit the ball, and make it pop over her foot and into the cup. She hit left-handed. She placed a match in front of a teed-up ball. When she hit the ball, the match exploded and sounded like a cannon. One of her favorite tricks was to tee up five balls and drive them one after the other, hitting the fifth ball before the first one landed. Babe's outgoing personality and humor provided a refreshing contrast to the serious concentration most other golfers brought to the game, and the galleries loved her.

Babe and Gene won most of their matches, thanks to Gene's golfing. Babe gained valuable experience by playing against some of the greatest golfers in the world. No one was good enough or famous enough to intimidate her.

Gene Sarazen, the first golfer to win four major men's championships, teamed up with Babe for a two-month tour in the summer of 1935.

She played against Joyce Wethered, who had won the British Women's Championship five years in a row. Wethered had retired from active competition, but beating her would greatly enhance Babe's reputation as a golfer. Inexplicably, Babe arranged an endorsement deal for golf clubs the night before the match and played with unfamiliar clubs. She lost the match, but not her confidence or her enthusiasm for golf.

Sarazen and Babe finished their tour in time for Babe to return to Texas for the Texas Open in October. The tournament was not her only challenge. Babe needed to overcome the hostile attitudes of Texas country-club society.

During her childhood and her early days in track and field, Babe's tough-girl appearance and attitude had worked to her advantage. For her new endeavor, the image had become a problem. When Babe arrived in Fort Worth to play in the Texas Open, she kept quiet and tried to shrug off the disapproval of the other golfers. Even so, the tense atmosphere seemed to bother her. Too many of her shots missed the cup, and she lost early in the tournament.

Bertha and R. L. Bowen had invited Babe to stay with them during the Texas Open. The tournament lasted only a few days—Babe stayed three weeks. At first she was intimidated by the Bowens' wealthy lifestyle. When she arrived for her stay with them, she sat outside in her car for a long time before she got up the nerve to go to the door.

Babe came to rely on the Bowens for encouragement and emotional support. At age twenty-four she was unrefined, uneducated, and accustomed to a life of traveling and living out of a suitcase—but she wasn't stupid. She began to realize that if she wanted to play golf, she would have to learn to play the social game. The Bowens introduced her to a quieter and more settled life, where good manners were important.

When Babe arrived at the Bowens' home, she had one good dress that she washed every night. Bertha Bowen let Babe borrow some of her dresses, then took her shopping. Babe had saved some of the money she made touring with Gene Sarazen and could buy the clothes she hadn't been able to afford as a teenager. She learned how to perm her hair and paint her nails.

Some of Babe's old friends were surprised at the changes in her after she came under the Bowens' influence. One reporter, who had not seen her since the Olympics, wrote, "I hardly knew Babe Didrikson when I saw her. Hair frizzed and she had a neat little wave in it, parted and prettily combed, a touch of rouge on her cheeks and red on her lips." The Texas Tomboy had grown up.

"I don't believe my personality has changed," Babe said. "I think anyone who knew me when I was a kid will tell you that I'm still the same Babe. It's just that as you get older, you're not as rambunctious as you used to be. You mellow down a bit." As if to prove that she was still the same, Babe decided her next tournament would be the Los Angeles Open. It was a regular event on the men's golf circuit for both professionals and amateurs. The Los Angeles Open had always been a men's tournament, but there was no rule that said women couldn't enter.

George Zaharias and Babe were interested in each other from the moment they met.

EIGHT

Romance

1938–1942

In January 1938, the Los Angeles Open rolled around. "I knew I wasn't going to beat the top men pros, but I was still trying to establish myself as the greatest woman golfer," she wrote in her autobiography. Babe was assigned two partners for the first two rounds. Both were good part-time golfers, but not in the same class as the real pros. One was Presbyterian minister C. Pardee Erdman, and the other was George Zaharias, a well-known professional wrestler.

"What an introduction George and I had!" Babe said. "One minute we were saying hello, and the next minute photographers were crowding around and calling for him to put wrestling holds on me. He put his arm around me, pretending to apply neck holds and stuff. And I didn't mind it at all."

George Zaharias was twenty-nine years old, 6 feet tall, and weighed more than 200 pounds. He had a tiny waist, huge hands, cauliflower ears, and shoulders so wide that he had to turn sideways to pass through narrow doorways. Like Babe, he exuded vitality and confidence.

Neither George nor Babe could concentrate on the golf game, and the minister beat them both. For most of Babe's life, sports had taken all her time and energy. She hadn't dated in high school and had had few crushes on men. But when she met George, she fell in love immediately. George was equally enchanted with Babe.

The eldest son of Greek immigrants, George had grown up in a one-room house in Pueblo, Colorado. As soon as he could, he worked to help support his family. He shined shoes, played pool for money, and did odd jobs. Later, he moved to Chicago and found a job as a wrestler making a dollar a day. Professional wrestling was a popular form of entertainment, and George was soon rich and famous.

He had size and wrestling skill, but it was his acting ability that made him successful in the ring. He played the bad guy who burst into tears when the good guy defeated him. Promoters described him as "the crying Greek from Cripple Creek." (Cripple Creek is a small town near Pueblo.) George was a smart businessman who knew how to promote himself and invest his money. He was making over $100,000 a year when he met Babe.

Babe and George began to date. She was busy playing exhibition matches during the day, and he had wrestling matches at night, but they made time to see each other. When George had a free night, he and Babe would go out for dinner and dancing.

George came to the driving ranges just to see Babe. Babe attended one of George's wrestling matches. She didn't like it. The crowds were wild, and the wrestling looked very rough. She was afraid George would get hurt. After a few weeks of steady dating, Babe introduced George to her mother—who, along with Lillie, had traveled with Babe to California for an extended visit, while Ole stayed in Beaumont. Hannah and George liked each other right away.

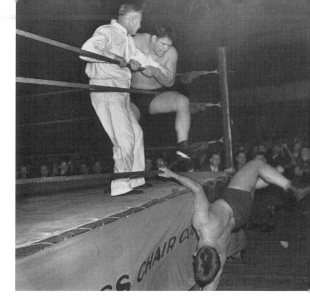

George, pictured in the ring, *made his fortune in professional wrestling.*

Eventually, Babe had to drive Hannah and Lillie back to Beaumont. George had wrestling dates in California. He and Babe promised to call and write to each other. Babe, Hannah, and Lillie left for Texas, but the farther away from California they drove, the worse Babe felt. By the time they stopped to visit her sister Dora in Phoenix, Babe was miserable. She was so unhappy about leaving George that she asked her mother and sister if they would mind continuing on to Beaumont by train. Then she drove back to California and George.

After a few months of dating, Babe and George decided they wanted to get married. They planned to have a big cele-bration with both of their families present, but conflicting schedules kept them from setting a date for the wedding. Finally, Babe and George found themselves together in St. Louis, Missouri. "George got real stern with me," Babe said. "He said, 'We're going to get married this week or call the whole deal off.'" They were married at the home of a mutual friend in St. Louis on December 23, 1938.

Because of their many professional obligations, the Zahariases didn't take a honeymoon until April 1939. Then they traveled to Australia and New Zealand. Always a smart businessman, George had arranged a series of wrestling matches and golf exhibitions in both countries. Babe was a hit in Australia. She dazzled everybody with her game and came within two strokes of beating the Australian men's champion.

When the Zahariases returned to the United States in the fall of 1939, George decided to quit wrestling so he could manage Babe's career. He was thirty and had fame and fortune. Babe was twenty-eight and still trying to establish herself as a professional golfer. As an athlete, George understood Babe's drive to excel and was willing to help her.

George and Babe were married by a justice of the peace in the St. Louis home of wrestling promoter Tom Packs.

The Zahariases traveled back and forth across the United States, promoting and holding golf clinics. The clinics and exhibition matches provided a good income, but no serious competition.

Babe began to reevaluate her future. She had developed a fine golf game, but since she was barred from amateur competition, about all she could do was play exhibition matches. The two tournaments a year that were open to female pros didn't provide enough opportunity for Babe to establish herself as a champion golfer. She missed the excitement of tournament golf and the thrill of playing her best and winning against a tough competitor.

When Babe was single, she had played sports professionally because she needed the money. When she married George, that problem ended. He was willing to support Babe and contribute money to her family as she had.

Babe and George decided the only way to get to the top in women's golf was as an amateur. According to USGA rules, she could be reinstated as an amateur if she had been professional for no more than five years. Babe met that requirement. Then she had to get four letters of endorsement from people prominent in amateur golf. She also had to submit to a three-year waiting period, during which she could not accept payment for playing golf or allow advertisers to use her name.

In January 1940, Babe dropped all her professional contracts and applied to the USGA to get her amateur status back. "I settled down to sweat it out," she said. "When I entered the occasional open tournament that I was eligible for, I told them to count me out on any prize money."

Babe's three years of waiting were happy ones. The Zahariases rented a house in Los Angeles. Babe had traveled a lot because her career demanded it, but she loved having a home. She cooked Norwegian meatballs and George's favorite Greek dishes. She decorated the house, sewed curtains, and tended a flower garden.

Babe's love of athletic competition was too strong to allow her to sit on the sidelines for long. She took up tennis again. Her old shoulder injury had healed, and Babe found she could play without pain. She tackled tennis with the same discipline and drive she used with golf. "When I go into a sport," Babe said, "I don't do it halfway." She hired Eleanor Tenant, who had taught Alice Marble and other champions, as her coach. They practiced at the Beverly Hills Tennis Club with tennis pros and movie stars. Sometimes Babe played seventeen sets a day, wearing out socks and sneakers frequently. Soon she was able to beat her coach. She started thinking about entering national doubles tournaments with Louise Brough, a leading tennis player.

George thought Babe was working too hard, but she had a plan. She wanted to enter the Southwest Tennis Championships in the fall of 1941. When she applied for the tournament, the United States Lawn Tennis Association rejected her for being a professional athlete. There were no provisions for Babe to ever regain her amateur standing in tennis.

Babe was disappointed. "Once I knew I could never compete in tournaments, that took the fun out of tennis for me. It's not enough for me just to play. I have to be able to try for championships," Babe said.

She stopped playing tennis and took up bowling. She took lessons and practiced far into the night in bowling alleys. She competed in various leagues and became known as one of the best amateur bowlers in Southern California.

Babe didn't neglect her golf game during these years.

She played several times a week, often with Hollywood stars. George joined her on the golf courses and in the bowling alleys. The Zahariases lived a sociable life in the early 1940s. They were an outgoing couple and made friends almost everywhere they went.

The world around them was going through difficult times. World War II had started in Europe. Germany invaded—then occupied—Poland, France, Holland, and Belgium. Italy and Japan were also exerting military force against other nations. At first, the United States was divided about sending help to Europe. Then on December 7, 1941, Japanese airplanes bombed the U.S. naval base at Pearl Harbor in the Hawaiian Islands. The United States had been drawn into the war. The country devoted its attention and resources to defeating Japan in the Pacific, and to fighting Germany and Italy in Europe. Many major sports events, including golf tournaments, were canceled.

The Zahariases also put their energy into supporting the U.S. war effort. George wanted to enlist in the armed services but was rejected because of his varicose veins. Babe promoted war bonds—the government's way of borrowing funds from individuals and businesses—by performing in celebrity golf exhibitions. She played with movie stars like Bing Crosby and Bob Hope and golf greats like Ben Hogan and Sam Snead. She kept up her golf game, helped the country, and entertained the galleries with her jokes and trick shots. Spectators loved her, and Babe had a great time.

Among her many accomplishments, Babe was credited with hitting a golf ball farther than any other woman.

NINE

A Record They'll Never Forget

1943–1947

On January 21, 1943, the United States Golf Association reinstated Babe as an amateur. She celebrated her return to amateur golf by playing in a charity match at the Desert Golf Club in Palm Springs. She shot a 70 on the first eighteen holes and a 67 on the second eighteen, breaking the women's record for the course and defeating the state champion, Clara Callender. For the next year and a half, while most tournaments were suspended because of the war, Babe continued to play in charity matches and minor tournaments in the Los Angeles area.

Despite Babe's accomplishments and success in golf, she also experienced some sadness. Babe's father, Ole Didriksen, died in 1943 as a result of cancer.

Babe played her first major tournament as an amateur at the 1944 Western Women's Open in Indianapolis, Indiana. She had won it as a professional in 1940, and she won it again as an amateur.

In 1945 George moved his wrestling promotion business from Los Angeles to Denver, Colorado. Between moving and settling into her new home, Babe returned to Indianapolis in

June to defend her title. No one had ever won the Western Open three times, and Babe wanted to be the first.

She won her first match. Then George called from Denver. Hannah Didriksen had suffered a heart attack in Los Angeles and was in critical condition. Babe wanted to fly home immediately. George dissuaded her. "Your Momma wants you to finish the tournament," he said.

Despite Babe's sorrow, she managed to win her quarterfinal match. Afterward, she tried to get to Los Angeles but could not find a seat on a plane or a train. The trains were full of troops, and the seats on the few commercial airlines were reserved for high-ranking military and government personnel. Gas was still being rationed because of the war, so she couldn't drive herself as far as Los Angeles.

The next day, Babe played in the semifinals and won. That evening, Esther Nancy called to tell Babe their mother had died. Babe wanted to withdraw from the tournament and return to Los Angeles immediately. But her sister said, "Go ahead and win that tournament. That's the way Momma would want it."

Babe was so upset that she couldn't speak to anybody. Instead, she consoled herself by playing harmonica for hours and hours. The next morning she shot a 72 to set a women's record for the course. She won the tournament, but it was a sad victory. In losing her mother, Babe had lost her greatest admirer.

Babe booked a seat on a plane and left for the West Coast early the next morning. The trip was long and hard. Babe lost her seat to a high-priority passenger in Kansas City, Missouri, and again in Albuquerque, New Mexico, and had to spend hours waiting in airports. Two days after starting her journey, Babe arrived in Los Angeles. Babe's brothers and sisters had delayed the funeral until she could get there. The family buried Hannah Didriksen on June 26, 1945—Babe's thirty-fourth birthday.

World War II ended in September of 1945, and the United States entered a period of economic prosperity. Americans had more leisure time and more money to spend on entertainment. Sports became increasingly popular. Golf tournaments that had been suspended during the war sprung up again.

Babe entered every tournament she could. In October she won the Texas Women's Open for the third time. In December, The Associated Press named her Woman Athlete of the Year. She had won the same award after her Olympic victories in 1932. "I got a special charge out of that 1945 award because it had been so many years since I'd had this recognition," she said.

In 1946 Babe won five tournaments in a row: the Trans-Mississippi Tournament in Denver, Colorado, the Broadmoor International in Colorado Springs, the All-American Championship in Niles, Illinois, the National Women's Amateur in Tulsa, Oklahoma, and the Texas Open. Babe loved having the opportunity to compete in so many tournaments, but she found the constant travel exhausting. Sometimes George accompanied her, but more often he stayed behind to tend his own business interests.

After winning the Texas Open, Babe wanted to relax and take a long break to enjoy her new house and rose garden in Denver, but George urged her to keep playing. "Honey," he said, "You've got something going here. You've won five straight tournaments. You want to build up that streak into a record they'll never forget." Babe followed George's advice and went to Florida to play in some early winter tournaments.

Some people claim that Babe won seventeen straight

tournaments during 1946 and 1947. No other golfer, male or female, has ever achieved such a record. Byron Nelson won eleven tournaments in a row. Sports historians would later dispute Babe's record, however. In September 1946, after thirteen straight wins, Babe lost the first round of the National Women's Open. Even with thirteen tournament wins in a row, Babe surpassed Byron Nelson's record. She came back to win the North and South Women's Amateur at Pinehurst, North Carolina. In 1946 The Associated Press again named her Woman Athlete of the Year.

Babe continued to win tournaments and came to dominate women's amateur golf. The golf course became her stage. She loved to compete, and she loved entertaining the crowds who came to see her play. She continued to perform her trick shots and to delight fans with her humor. When one of her long drives went into the rough, she would turn to the gallery and explain, "I hit it straight, but it went crooked."

Babe also changed the game of women's golf. Her long, powerful drives gave her a tremendous advantage over her competitors and drew many spectators. She dominated the women's circuit. In order to compete against her, other golfers began to imitate her.

By the middle of the 1947 season, Babe had won fourteen tournaments and lost only one. She enjoyed her victories, but she was also restless. At thirty-five, she was at the top of her game and in top physical condition. She wanted to be the best golfer in the world, and she knew other famous golfers— Walter Hagen, Bobby Jones, and Gene Sarazen—had all added to their reputations by winning British championships.

At the time, the British Women's Amateur was considered by many golfers to be the best women's tournament in the world. Since its beginning in 1893, no one from the United

States had ever won there. Babe decided to enter, and she was determined to win it. "There never was an event that was more important for me in sports than the British Women's Amateur golf championship," she wrote later.

George was occupied with business dealings, so Babe traveled to Gullane, Scotland, alone. Just getting to Gullane proved challenging. Babe took a boat to Southampton, England, a train to London, and another train to Edinburgh, Scotland. Babe was loaded down with suitcases and cameras, and the trains were overcrowded. She had to stand for most of the ten-hour train ride from London to Edinburgh.

Once Babe arrived in Gullane, a seaside town in northern Scotland, she was treated like an honored guest. Despite food rationing in Great Britain after World War II, the manager of the Berwick Inn had managed to stock up on some of Babe's favorite foods—bacon, eggs, and potatoes. The Scots

Babe at the conclusion of the 1945 Texas Women's Golf Open. She received two trophies, one for being a medalist in the qualifying round and the other for winning the Open.

were warm and friendly, and they made Babe feel right at home. Golf had originated in Scotland sometime during the fourteenth century and has always been a well-loved sport there. The local people watched Babe practice from their houses near the fairways, and they greeted her warmly when she walked around the town. Babe accepted many invitations to tea.

The tournament was scheduled to start on June 9. Babe had arrived a few days early to familiarize herself with the golf course. Even though George phoned her daily and urged her not to do too much practicing, she stayed on the course for hours.

The golf course at Gullane was different from American tournament courses. "There were sheep wandering all over the place . . . ," Babe recalled. "When I came along in a practice round, the sheep would just step aside. . . ."

On her second practice round, Babe hit her ball into some tall, wet grass off the fairway. Babe hit the ball out of the rough, but her club had gotten tangled in the grass on the shot. The handle banged Babe's left thumb and chipped a bone. "I didn't want anybody to think I was trying to build up an advance alibi for myself, so I just wore a glove over it, and nobody noticed that there was anything the matter with my thumb," she said. Babe thought her sore thumb improved her game. She couldn't slug the ball as far, so she had more control of her shots.

But she wasn't prepared for the weather. Even in the summertime it could change from sunny and warm to cold and wet in a few hours. Soon after Babe arrived, the weather became cold and wet. She had packed only light summer clothes. When word got out that Babe needed warm clothes, local people sent her bundles of heavy clothing. The hotel lobby was stacked with such gifts. Babe picked out a pair of slacks and a jumpsuit and wrote thank you notes for those two items. She asked the newspaper reporters to publish her thanks to everybody else and had the rest of the clothing sent back.

The tournament started on Monday, June 9. The ninety-nine women were assigned partners at random. They would play two eighteen-hole matches each day, one in the morning and one in the afternoon, until only two players remained. The finalists would compete in a thirty-six-hole match on Thursday. Babe won her first round easily, but the quietness of the crowd bothered her. The gallery murmured after every shot and sometimes applauded politely. "I wish these people would holler and enjoy themselves the way the crowds do back home," Babe said. An official explained that Scottish tradition dictated the gallery be very quiet to keep from disturbing the players. Babe wanted to loosen up the crowd.

In the afternoon, she began to joke with the gallery. "I told them they could make all the noise they wanted to and it wouldn't bother me. I said the noise would make me play better, because it was what I was used to." Babe won her afternoon match and then did a few of her trick shots for the audience. The crowd loved her antics.

Not everyone appreciated Babe's tricks and flamboyant ways. Some ladies complained to Mrs. A. M. Holm, a British golfer and a quarterfinalist in the tournament. They thought Babe was boastful, vulgar, and lacking refinement. "You are speaking of the finest woman golfer that has ever been seen here," Holm replied.

Babe defeated one opponent after another. In the final round, she faced the British golfer Jaqueline Gordon. When they began to play in the morning, the weather was warm and sunny. Babe wore her summer clothes and an old pair of golf

Babe, left, *and Jean Donald,* right, *danced a highland fling after the semifinal match in the British Women's Amateur golf championship in 1947.*

shoes. Her favorite pair had begun to split from the dampness, so she left them in her hotel room. The weather changed halfway through the first eighteen holes. It grew windy, and Babe began to shiver. Jaqueline Gordon maintained her concentration and continued to play well. The cold weather didn't seem to bother her. At the end of the first round, the score was tied.

During the lunch break, Babe went back to her hotel for warm clothes and her favorite shoes, which she wanted to have repaired for the final round. All the stores were closed because of the tournament. Word circulated that Babe was looking for someone to fix her shoes. The local shoemaker found Babe and repaired her shoes before the afternoon round began.

In the final round, Babe took the lead at the first hole and kept it for the rest of the match. Jaqueline Gordon won only one hole all afternoon. Babe secured a five-hole lead with four holes left. (Since Gordon then had no chance to tie or win, the match was over.) Babe had won the tournament! The crowd gave her a fifteen-minute ovation. Babe signed autographs and entertained the crowds by dancing a Highland fling. During the trophy presentation, she delighted everyone by singing a Scottish song.

After touring and playing a few of Scotland's most renowned golf courses, Babe sailed back to the United States aboard the *Queen Elizabeth,* the most luxurious ocean liner of the day. Three hours before it reached Manhattan, a tugboat approached the ship. "As their boat got close, I could see a big guy with a white shirt standing up front at the rail. I said, 'That's George!' And it was," Babe wrote.

The Zahariases spent a few days in New York, talking to reporters and celebrating before flying home to Denver. The city gave her a huge victory parade. Babe rode on a float and threw roses into the crowd. The governor of Colorado, the mayor of Denver, and fifty thousand people turned out to cheer the first American to win the British Women's Amateur Championship.

Babe was an important figure in founding the Ladies Professional Golf Association (LPGA).

TEN

The Birth of the LPGA

1947–1951

In July 1947, Babe won the Broadmoor Match Play Tournament in Colorado Springs—reportedly her seventeenth tournament win in a row. With the excitement over Babe's victory at the British Women's Amateur, her defeat in the 1946 National Women's Open had been forgotten.

Everyone celebrated her record-setting winning streak of seventeen tournament victories. Babe was one of the most famous people in the United States. Promoters and advertisers offered her huge sums of money if she would again turn professional.

Babe didn't need the money. George's wrestling and business ventures continued to be profitable, and he could afford to support her on the amateur golf circuit. Nevertheless, some of the offers were tempting. Fred Corcoran, promotional director of the men's Professional Golfers Association, wanted to represent her if she turned professional. A movie company offered her $300,000 to make ten short films on golf.

Babe began to realize that she could make a lot of money if she turned professional. She had risen to the top in amateur golf. She was ready for a new challenge. The movie offer was too good to refuse. Babe decided to turn pro again. "It nearly killed me to throw over the amateur standing I'd struggled so hard to get, but I couldn't see any other choice," she said in her autobiography.

Babe hired Fred Corcoran. In August Babe and Corcoran held a press conference in New York to announce that she was turning professional again. A reporter asked her where she was going to play golf, since there were still very few women's tournaments open to professionals. Corcoran later remembered how Babe's flair for publicity took over. " 'Well,' [Babe] said, 'I'm going to enter the U.S. Open Championship—for *men*.' I didn't know she was going to say this. I don't think she did when she got up there. There was this stunned silence, mouths dropped, and then the press—en masse—made a dash for the phones." The next morning, newspapers across the country carried details of Babe's announcement. That same day, the USGA barred women from the U.S. Open.

The movie deal fell through too. Babe wasn't disappointed by these setbacks, because other opportunities came. She signed a lifetime contract with the Wilson Sporting Goods Company for a line of Babe Zaharias golf equipment. Serbin dress manufacturers agreed to make a golf dress Babe designed. Babe published a book on how to play golf. And she hit the road again.

Fred Corcoran booked her into major league baseball stadiums all over the country for $500 a night. Babe would play third base during batting practice and hit golf balls into the outfield. She seldom saw her home in Denver. "The fees were good," Babe wrote in her autobiography, "but we probably booked too many of them. One month there were seventeen nights that I was on a plane."

In October 1947, Babe lost in the quarterfinals of the Texas Women's Open, the first tournament of her new professional career. The press reported the end of Babe's tournament winning streak at seventeen.

Babe bounced back and won her next tournament, the Hardscrabble Women's Open in Little Rock, Arkansas. Babe's score of 293 strokes over seventy-two holes set a world record low score for women. In 1947 The Associated Press named her Woman Athlete of the Year for the third year in a row.

Babe continued to win tournaments throughout 1948. She was thirty-seven years old, the greatest female golfer in the world, and one of the wealthiest—but she was also unhappy and frustrated. She was again facing the same dilemma she had when she first started playing golf in the 1930s. There were few women's tournaments open to professionals. Only six women played professionally. Patty Berg was the only other pro who played regularly. Like Babe, she had a contract with the Wilson Sporting Goods Company and played golf exhibitions all over the country. It became obvious to Babe and George that women needed more professional tournaments, more prize money, and an organization dedicated to promoting women's golf.

In January 1949, Babe, George, Fred Corcoran, and Patty Berg met in Florida and spent two afternoons laying the groundwork for the Ladies Professional Golf Association (LPGA). Berg volunteered to be the association's first president. Corcoran did most of the actual organizing, finding sponsors for new tournaments and setting up the competitions. L. B. Icely, president of Wilson Sporting Goods Company, agreed to put up the prize money.

The LPGA started slowly. At first, it had just six members. The organization held nine tournaments and awarded fifteen thousand dollars in prize money. Even so, the LPGA started a new era in women's golf. With a regular professional tournament schedule and an organization dedicated to promoting women's golf, dozens more women turned professional during the LPGA's first year. Babe garnered a ton of publicity for the tournaments and the tour, and she almost always attended LPGA functions to mingle with and entertain sponsors and reporters.

In the early years of the LPGA, Babe was the leading money winner and the most famous player on the tour. In 1950 she won two-thirds of the tournaments and $14,800 in prize money. Her presence on the tour, more than anything else, helped the LPGA succeed. Patty Berg recalled Babe's importance to the LPGA in those early days:

> Babe changed the game of golf for women—not only by bringing along the LPGA, but by her kind of golf. She came along with that great power game and it led to lower scores and more excitement. She even changed the swing. . . . We hit waist high, more flat. Babe would swing high and hard. And she brought all that humor and showmanship to the game. She humanized it. She was the happiest girl you ever saw, like a kid. Our sport grew because of Babe, because she had so much flair and color. Her tremendous enthusiasm for golf and life was contagious—even the galleries felt good when Babe was around.

The qualities Patty Berg admired caused many other women on the tour to resent Babe. To some, Babe's self-confidence came across as arrogance. Babe loved to win, and at times her fierce competitiveness could unnerve her opponents. She would stride into a locker room and call out, "Okay, Babe's here! Now who's gonna finish second?"

Patty Berg, right, *beat Babe by five strokes in the 1946 Women's National Open golf tournament.*

Babe claimed to have mellowed as she grew older, but she was still blunt and outspoken, and she still liked to play practical jokes. When she was playing on the tour, she would put a hairbrush in her roommate's bed, disguise her voice on the telephone, or hide under her roommate's bed and grab her foot as she started to fall asleep. Some of the women on the tour found these pranks crude and her frankness embarrassing. Babe had an exuberant personality, though, and most people who knew her loved her.

While she was the star of the LPGA tour, Babe was also involved in other moneymaking adventures. She played exhibition matches, did promotional events, and taught golf—first at Grossinger's in New York, and then at the Sky Crest Country Club near Chicago. In 1950 Babe received one of the greatest honors of her career: The Associated Press named her Greatest Female Athlete of the Half-Century.

In 1951 Babe turned forty. That same year, Babe and George bought the Forest Country Club in Tampa, Florida.

They renamed it the Tampa Golf and Country Club and converted a caddie shack into their home. Babe wanted to stay in Tampa to decorate and garden, but golf kept her on the road, away from her new home and away from George.

Over the years, Babe and George grew apart. George had his own business ventures and was often too busy to go with Babe when she traveled. He loved to pack himself into his Cadillac and drive off for weeks at a time, looking after his investments or just traveling around the countryside. George's appearance was another sore spot between them. After George retired from wrestling, his compulsive eating and drinking caused him to gain weight steadily, and he grew to more than four hundred pounds.

The Zahariases never had children. Babe suffered at least one miscarriage, but if she regretted not having children she

Betty Dodd, left, *and Babe,* right, *often entertained their fellow golfers after a day of golfing.*

rarely talked about it. Perhaps the responsibilities of raising a family would have interfered with her drive to be the best golfer in the world.

As the years passed, Babe grew more and more independent of George. She no longer depended on him for advice, as she had during the early days of their marriage. He came to resent her success and the new friends she made through golf. And while Babe's career continued to soar, George had difficulties with his business investments. Sometimes Babe and George fought and talked of separating, but they never divorced. They maintained a public image of happiness and harmony.

While the Zahariases were living in Tampa, Babe met nineteen-year-old Betty Dodd. Betty was a tall redhead from a well-to-do family. She had been golfing since she was thirteen and was a rising star in the world of golf. Betty had seen Babe play in 1947 and idolized her. Bertha Bowen had written to Babe asking her to take Betty under her wing.

Soon Betty was staying with the Zahariases in Tampa. The two women developed a close friendship and became inseparable. They traveled to tournaments together and shared many of the same interests, such as making music. Betty sang and played guitar while Babe accompanied her on harmonica.

Babe continued to dominate the tour. In 1951 she was again the leading money winner. She won seven of the twelve tournaments she played. "When I didn't win a tournament, I'd almost always be second or third, no worse than fourth or fifth," Babe said. "Nobody can be first in all of them, of course, with competition as tough as it is in women's golf today."

*Babe, right, and Patty Berg, left, kiss a putter after Babe won the 1950
All-American golf tournament in the women's professional division.*

ELEVEN

The Last Round

1952–1956

As the 1952 season began, Babe's career continued to soar. She either won or finished near the top in every tournament she played. She was so famous that she landed a small part in the film *Pat and Mike,* starring Katherine Hepburn and Spencer Tracy.

Babe was forty years old and proud of her strong, healthy body. Although she had rarely been ill, Babe had been bothered by intermittent pain and swelling in her left side for several years. In May 1952, the pain had become so constant and so bad that she went to Dr. W. E. Tatum, her family doctor in Beaumont. He diagnosed a hernia and operated almost immediately. After a short rest, Babe went back to playing golf. She was feeling fine and doing well in tournaments. By November, though, she felt tired all the time and had to drag herself around the golf course. Finally, in April 1953, she went back to Dr. Tatum after winning a tournament in Beaumont.

"I could see his face out of the corner of my eye," Babe said. "All of a sudden he just turned white. He didn't say a word. I guess I'd suspected all along what my trouble was. I said to him, 'I've got cancer, haven't I?'"

Dr. Tatum sent Babe to a specialist in Fort Worth, Texas, who confirmed the diagnosis: rectal cancer. Babe would need to undergo a colostomy—an operation to remove the cancer and reroute the lower end of her digestive system. When the surgery was over, Babe would have an opening in her left side where body waste could be removed. The diagnosis and recommended treatment came as a shock to Babe. At first she despaired. "What in the world have I done wrong in my life to deserve this?" she thought. She tried to give away her golf clubs because she thought she wouldn't need them anymore, but George wouldn't let her.

Babe's surgery took place on April 17, 1953. The operation was successful, but surgeons discovered that the cancer had spread to Babe's lymph nodes. They couldn't operate on lymphatic cancer. George, Betty Dodd, and Babe's other close friends decided not to tell her that she had inoperable cancer.

Betty slept on a cot in Babe's hospital room and helped nurse her through her recuperation. George was constantly at Babe's side. Letters and telegrams poured in from people around the world wishing Babe a speedy recovery. Her bag of golf clubs stood in the corner, inspiring her to get well.

As Babe recovered from the operation, she began to worry about her golf career. The surgery had radically changed her body, and she wondered if she would ever be able to compete again in tournaments. Her optimism and determination soon conquered her worry. "All my life I've been competing—and competing to win. I came to realize that in its way, this cancer was the toughest competition I'd faced yet. I made up my mind that I was going to lick it all the way. I not only wasn't going to let it kill me, I wasn't even going to let it put me on the shelf. I was determined to come back and win golf championships just the same as before."

Ten days after the surgery, Babe was up on her feet, visiting other patients in the hospital and cheering them up. When Babe left the hospital on May 18, she had recovered some of her strength, but her doctors still thought she would never play professional tournament golf again.

Babe tried a bit of golfing during the next months, increasing the amount little by little. With her doctors' permission, she decided to try a tournament. She entered the All-American golf tournament at the Tam O'Shanter Country Club near Chicago. It took place less than four months after her operation. Betty Dodd was paired with Babe every round in case she needed help. Nervous and fearful of injuring herself, she played cautiously. She had to sit and rest after every shot while George massaged her back and shoulders. Even though Babe remained weak and stiff from the surgery, she still had her sense of humor. "Man, if I hit any better it would kill me," she joked when she smacked a 250-yard drive.

On the first nine holes, she was always in trouble and frequently landed in sand traps. She finished the first round with a score of 82. On the second day, her shots went wild and she often missed her putts. But the third day was the most difficult. Babe was exhausted and in pain. When she missed an easy shot on the fifth hole, she sat down, put her face in her hands, and cried. Betty and George urged her to go back to the clubhouse. They said everyone would understand if she quit. Babe refused to withdraw, though, and she finished the tournament in fifteenth place.

She was back on the same golf course days later, taking third in the World Golf Championship. She continued playing the rest of the season. As much as Babe loved to play golf, it wasn't easy. She hadn't recovered all her strength and was often tired and sore.

Babe was overjoyed when she left the John Sealy Memorial Hospital after her four-month fight with a second occurrence of cancer.

Her courage and perseverance were inspiring. When people asked her why she didn't retire, Babe replied, "One reason is that every time I get out and play well in a golf tournament it seems to buck up people with the same cancer trouble I had."

The LPGA was another reason Babe kept playing. She thought the tournaments drew more people if all the players on the tour participated. As its president and one of the founding members, she wanted to keep it growing. By 1953, there were twenty tournaments on the tour and $225,000 in prize money. Babe was given the Ben Hogan Comeback of the Year award that year.

In 1954 Babe was more her usual self. She won five tournaments, including a twelve-stroke win at the Women's Open. The Associated Press named her Outstanding Woman Athlete of the Year for the sixth time. She was winning again, but she admitted that she didn't have the stamina that she had had before the surgery. By the fourth round, she would struggle to play at her usual level.

Neither Babe nor her family had attended church regularly, but Babe began to look to religion as a source of strength and support. "I promised God that if He made me well, I'd do everything in my power when I got out to help the fight against cancer," Babe said. She made personal appearances and did radio and television spots to raise money for cancer research.

In 1954 she went to the White House in Washington, D.C., to meet President Dwight D. Eisenhower and to open the annual Cancer Crusade. Babe and Eisenhower, both avid golfers, struck up a friendship right away. In her autobiography, Babe recalled their first meeting. "He shook hands with me, and I said, 'How do you do, Mr. President.' He said, 'How do you do, Mrs. Zaharias.' Then he dropped his head and pretended to whisper. 'I'll see you later, Babe,' he said. 'I want to talk to you about this game of golf.'"

Early in 1955, Babe's strength and energy began to fade again. She took a vacation with Betty Dodd to the Gulf of Mexico for a spring fishing trip. They had a wonderful time fishing and relaxing in the sun. Babe began to feel better. Then they ran into some bad luck. One day, Betty's car got stuck in the sand. They borrowed a shovel, and Babe went to work trying to dig the wheels out of the sand. The next day, she awoke later with incredible back pain. "Now that I look back," Betty Dodd later said, "this was the beginning of the end. The cancer had returned, but it took *months* to find it."

Babe and Betty returned home. Despite her constant pain, Babe continued to play in tournaments, winning the Tampa Open, the Serbin Women's Open, and the Peach Blossom–Betsy Rawls Open. When the pain became unbearable, Babe entered the hospital again. After repeated examinations, doctors finally found cancer in her lower spine. They couldn't operate, so at the end of July they sent Babe home to Tampa with painkillers.

Betty Dodd and George continued to care for her. Babe played a little golf and worked on her autobiography. She would begin to feel like her old self again, but then the pain would return. Sometimes it was so intense, she could hardly stand. In March 1956, she was admitted to a hospital in Galveston, Texas. Betty wanted to stay with her, but Babe thought Betty had spent enough time being a nurse. Babe insisted that Betty go back to playing golf on the LPGA tour, and she called her sister Lillie to come and stay with her.

Babe never was a quitter. Even at the end of her life, she did not give up easily. It took months for the cancer to defeat her. When Babe died on September 27, 1956, she was forty-five years old. She was buried near her parents in Beaumont, Texas.

The world mourned Babe's passing. All kinds of people— ordinary and famous—sent cards, telegrams, and flowers. President Eisenhower interrupted a press conference to pay tribute to her. "Ladies and gentlemen," he said, "I should like to take one minute to pay a tribute to Mrs. Zaharias, Babe Didrikson. She was a woman, who in her athletic career, certainly won the admiration of every person in the United States, all sports people all over the world, and in her gallant fight against cancer, she put up one of the kind of fights that inspired us all. I think that every one of us feels sad that finally she had to lose this last one of all her battles."

After her death, people continued to recognize Babe for her achievements. In 1968 she was one of the first four women inducted into the LPGA Hall of Fame. She was also inducted into the National Track and Field Hall of Fame in 1974. Hollywood released a movie called *Babe* in 1975. She was honored on a commemorative stamp, one of the few women to receive this recognition, in 1981. Many of Babe's medals and trophies are on display at the Babe Didrikson Zaharias Museum in Beaumont, Texas.

Many people acclaim Babe as the greatest American athlete ever. Her excellence in so many sports—baseball, basketball, diving, tennis, bowling, and golf—makes her the most versatile athlete the United States has ever produced.

Babe believed in herself and prided herself in her own accomplishments. She didn't think of herself as a role model for other women, nor did she concern herself with women's issues. At a time when professional female athletes had few opportunities and were regarded as abnormal or "muscle molls," Babe refused to be discouraged. She pursued her goal of being the world's greatest athlete with courage, determination, and discipline. Even when her athletic career was halted over issues of amateurism and professionalism, Babe clung to her dreams.

Babe Didrikson Zaharias also left a living legacy. She changed women's golf tremendously. Her long drives enabled her to go around a golf course with fewer strokes. Other golfers had to copy her in order to compete. Babe's flamboyant personality and her gift for entertaining the tournament crowds increased the popularity of the sport. By helping to form the LPGA, Babe opened doors for other women in professional golf. She left many of her contemporaries with fond memories.

Patty Berg, Babe's friend and competitor, once said, "Sometimes I find myself leaning back in a chair thinking about Babe, and I have to smile—with Babe there was never a dull moment."

Babe throwing the javelin in 1932, the same year she was first named Woman Athlete of the Year

Sources

p. 8   Babe Didrikson Zaharias, with Harry Paxton, *This Life I've Led* (San Diego: A. S. Barnes & Company, 1955), 45.

p. 9   Elizabeth A. Lynn, *Babe Didrikson Zaharias: Champion Athlete* (New York: Chelsea House Publishers, 1989), 14.

p. 10   Zaharias, *This Life I've Led*, 48.

p. 10   Ibid., 49.

p. 11   Ibid., 50.

p. 14   Ibid., 27.

p. 15   Ibid., 11.

p. 17   Ibid., 20.

p. 18   Ibid., 25.

p. 18   Ibid., 22.

p. 19   Ibid., 15.

p. 19   Ibid., 16.

p. 21   William Oscar Johnson and Nancy P. Williamson, *Whatta-Gal: The Babe Didrikson Story* (Boston: Little, Brown, 1975), 58.

p. 22   Zaharias, *This Life I've Led*, 33.

p. 22   Johnson, *Whatta-Gal*, 25.

p. 23   Ibid., 54.

p. 25   Zaharias, *This Life I've Led*, 28.

p. 26   Johnson, *Whatta-Gal*, 56.

p. 27   Zaharias, *This Life I've Led*, 35.

p. 27   Johnson, *Whatta-Gal*, 64.

p. 28   Zaharias, *This Life I've Led*, 3.

p. 29   Ibid., 36.

p. 29   Ibid., 37.

p. 29   Babe Didrikson Zaharias, letter to Bill (Tiny) Scurlock, January 19, 1932, Babe Didrikson Zaharias Collection, Mary and John Gray Library, Lamar University, Beaumont, Texas.

p. 31   Zaharias, *This Life I've Led*, 39.

p. 32   Ibid., 43.

p. 33   Zaharias, letter to Scurlock, March 6, 1930.

p. 33   Johnson, *Whatta-Gal*, 75.

p. 33   Zaharias, letter to Scurlock, October 5, 1931.

p. 34   Zaharias, *This Life I've Led*, 40.

p. 34   Ibid.

pp. 34–35   Ibid., 41.

p. 36   Ibid., 42.

p. 36   Johnson, *Whatta-Gal*, 73.

p. 37   Bill Cunningham, "Texas Flash," *Collier's*, August 16, 1932, 49.

p. 37   Ibid.

p. 40   Zaharias, *This Life I've Led*, 52.

p. 42   Susan E. Cayleff, *Babe: The Life and Legend of Babe Didrikson Zaharias* (Chicago: University of Illinois Press, 1995), 73.

p. 42   Johnson, *Whatta-Gal*, 100.

p. 42   Ibid., 103.

p. 43   Ibid., 104.

p. 44   Zaharias, *This Life I've Led*, 56.

p. 46   R. R. Knudson, *Babe Didrikson: Athlete of the Century* (New York: Puffin, 1985), 36.

p. 46   Johnson, *Whatta-Gal*, 137.

p. 49   Frank Menke, "Intimate Glimpses of the Olympic Miracle, 'Babe' Didrikson," *Denver Post*, October 23, 1932, 7.

p. 50   Johnson, *Whatta-Gal*, 116.

p. 51   Zaharias, *This Life I've Led*, 69.

p. 52   Ibid., 73.

p. 53   Ibid., 77.

pp. 54–55   Ibid., 79.

p. 55   Johnson, *Whatta-Gal*, 132.

p. 57   Zaharias, *This Life I've Led*, 85.

p. 57   Ibid., 86.

p. 58   Ibid., 87.

p. 58   Johnson, *Whatta-Gal*, 141.

p. 58   Zaharias, *This Life I've Led*, 88.

p. 59   Rhonda Glenn, *The Illustrated History of Women's Golf* (Dallas: Taylor Publishing Co., 1991), 136.

p. 60   Zaharias, *This Life I've Led*, 93.

pp. 61–62   Ibid., 95–96.

p. 62   Ibid., 96.

p. 63   Ibid., 98.

p. 63 Johnson, *Whatta-Gal*, 147.

p. 64 Ibid.

p. 64 Zaharias, *This Life I've Led*, 98.

p. 64 Gene Schoor, *Babe Didrikson Zaharias: World's Greatest Woman Athlete* (Garden City, New York: Doubleday, 1978), 93.

pp. 64–65 Zaharias, *This Life I've Led*, 100.

p. 67 Johnson, *Whatta-Gal*, 153.

p. 67 Zaharias, *This Life I've Led*, 104.

p. 69 Ibid., 104.

p. 69 Ibid., 105.

p. 71 Ibid., 111.

p. 73 Ibid., 120.

p. 74 Ibid., 124.

p. 74 Ibid., 125.

p. 78 Ibid., 136.

p. 78 Ibid., 137.

p. 79 Ibid., 139.

p. 79 Ibid., 142.

p. 80 Cayleff, *Babe*, 163.

p. 81 Zaharias, *This Life I've Led,* 149.

p. 82 Ibid., 154–155.

p. 82 Ibid., 157.

p. 83 Ibid., 162.

p. 83 Ibid.

p. 83 Johnson, *Whatta-Gal*, 178.

p. 85 Zaharias, *This Life I've Led*, 177.

p. 88 Ibid., 180.

p. 88 Johnson, *Whatta-Gal*, 183.

p. 88 Zaharias, *This Life I've Led*, 182.

p. 90 Johnson, *Whatta-Gal*, 190–191.

p. 90 Ibid., 192.

p. 93 Zaharias, *This Life I've Led*, 190.

p. 95 Ibid., 197.

p. 96 Ibid., 201.

p. 96 Ibid., 5.

p. 97 "Babe is Back," *Time*, August 10, 1953, 44.

p. 98 Zaharias, *This Life I've Led*, 228.

p. 99 Ibid., 224.

p. 99 Ibid., 222.

p. 99 Johnson, *Whatta-Gal*, 211.

p. 100 "The Transcript of Eisenhower's News Conference," *New York Times*, September 28, 1956, 14.

p. 101 Johnson, *Whatta-Gal*, 190.

Selected Bibliography

Books

Cayleff, Susan E. *Babe: The Life and Legend of Babe Didrikson Zaharias*. Chicago: University of Illinois Press, 1995.

Freedman, Russell. *Babe Didrikson Zaharias: The Making of a Champion*. New York: Clarion, 1999.

Glenn, Rhonda. *The Illustrated History of Women's Golf*. Dallas: Taylor Publishing Co., 1991.

Johnson, William Oscar, and Nancy P. Williamson. *Whatta-Gal: The Babe Didrikson Story*. Boston: Little, Brown, 1975.

Knudson, R. R. *Babe Didrikson: Athlete of the Century*. New York: Puffin, 1985.

Lynn, Elizabeth A. *Babe Didrikson Zaharias: Champion Athlete*. New York: Chelsea House Publishers, 1989.

Schoor, Gene. *Babe Didrikson Zaharias: World's Greatest Woman Athlete*. Garden City, New York: Doubleday, 1978.

Zaharias, Babe Didrikson, with Harry Paxton. *This Life I've Led*. San Diego: A. S. Barnes & Company, 1955.

Magazines and Newspaper Articles

Babe Didrikson Zaharias Collection. Mary and John Gray Library, Lamar University, Beaumont, Texas.

"Babe Is Back." *Time,* August 10, 1953, 44.

Cunningham, Bill. "Texas Flash." *Collier's*, August 16, 1932, 49.

Menke, Frank. "Intimate Glimpses of the Olympic Miracle, 'Babe' Didrikson." *Denver Post*, October 23, 1932, 7.

"The Transcript of Eisenhower's News Conference." *New York Times*, September 28, 1956, 14.

"Camera-Shy but Carefree, Miss Didrikson Moves on toward Career as a Pro." *New York Times*, December 24, 1932, 19.

Index

Eighteen-year-old Babe Didrikson practices her high jump at Dyche Stadium in Evanston, Illinois.

Babe practicing her golf swing in 1937.

107

Throughout her lifetime, Babe won many trophies and medals. Here, she clutches the trophy she won at the British Women's Amateur golf championship.

About the Author

Nancy Wakeman was born in Boston, Massachusetts, and grew up in a small town by the ocean. Her parents encouraged her in sports, and she learned a lot about competition and cooperation through playing team sports. Later, she attended Hollins College and George Washington University, where she earned a master's degree in education. Nancy has worked as a social worker, secretary, counselor, child care worker, and candlemaker. She lives in San Francisco, California, and is a full-time writer.

Photo Acknowledgments

The photographs and illustrations are reproduced with the permission of: UPI/Corbis-Bettmann pp. 2, 9, 30, 35, 38, 40, 41, 45, 53, 54, 56, 60, 63, 71–72, 76, 81, 84, 86, 91, 92, 94, 102, 106, 107, 108; Archive Photos p. 6; Archive Photos/APA pp. 65, 68; Babe Didrikson Zaharias Collection, John Gray Library, Lamar University pp. 12, 16–17, 24 32; Seth Poppel Yearbook Archives 20; Corbis-Bettmann pp. 48, 100.

Cover: UPI/Corbis-Bettmann